THE
KNIGHTS
TEMPLAR

IN

YORKSHIRE

THE
KNIGHTS
TEMPLAR
IN
YORKSHIRE

DIANE HOLLOWAY & TRISH COLTON

First published 2008

Reprinted 2008, 2009, 2010, 2011, 2012

The History Press
The Mill, Brimscombe Port
Stroud, Gloucestershire, GL5 2QG
www.thehistorypress.co.uk

British Library Cataloguing in Publication Data.
A catalogue record for this book is available from the British Library.

ISBN 978 0 7509 5087 9

Typeset in 10.5/13pt Sabon.
Typesetting and origination by
The History Press.
Printed and bound in England.

CONTENTS

ACKNOWLEDGEMENTS

We owe particular thanks to the following people and organisations: Dr Evelyn Lord; West Yorkshire Archaeological Services; Humber Archaeology Partnership; Nick Boldrini, Historic Environment Record Officer, Heritage and Environment Section, NorthYorkshire County Council; Dr John Walker, University of Hull; the Patchett family; John Lee; the Nutt family; John and Jean Taylor; John Rushton; Irene Szymanski; and Jonathan Young.

We have also benefited enormously from the fruits of other people's labours in the form of published research carried out over centuries, as our bibliography shows.

Unless otherwise indicated, all pictures are our own. However, we should like to acknowledge the courtesy extended to us by the following, who allowed us to their pictures and illustrations: Simon Brighton, I. Szymanski, Wetherby Historical Trust, Yorkshire Archaeological Society, and Jonathan Young.

Finally, thank you to our mother, Dorothy Taylor, for her confidence in us and her financial support for our research and to our children, for almost managing to stifle their yawns when we ranted on about what we were doing, but reading our chapters for us anyway.

Stained glass window in Ribston's Templar chapel showing a Knight Templar. (Courtesy of Simon Brighton)

FOREWORD

The year 2007 marked the 700th anniversary of the arrest of the Knights Templar in France. The arrests of the British Templars followed in January 1308, so it is fitting that a new book on the Order of the Poor Knights of Christ of the Temple of Solomon in England should be published this year – the British 700th anniversary. Although the Knights Templars' role was primarily to protect pilgrims in the Holy Land, they soon became part of a mission to keep the Holy Land, and especially Jerusalem, in Christian hands. In order to do this they needed manpower and money, and to this end they came West to seek recognition of their Order and resources to fund it. Kings, nobles and churchmen responded by giving them estates, and the Templars quickly became significant landowners in France, Iberia and England.

An important part of their land in England lay in Yorkshire, and in this book Diane Holloway and Trish Colton have presented an in-depth study of the Knights Templars in that county, life in their preceptories and the society that lay outside them. They have identified ten preceptories and visited the sites of all of them. Their descriptions of the topography in which the preceptories are set place the Templars into the landscape in a way that only someone with an intimate knowledge of a county can do. Archaeological and documentary evidence is drawn together so that the preceptory buildings rise from the ruins and the Templars themselves inhabit them.

The lives of the Templars are described in detail. As appropriate for a military religious order, warfare and weaponry are discussed in detail, as is the Church and pilgrimage, demonstrating the Order's less war-like role. The background to their role as farmers and landlords appears, and the reader learns about medieval agriculture, mills, forests, and land law. Education, crime and punishment, medicine, architecture and trade in the Templars' time are also described. Although the Templars were an exclusively male order, they had many women tenants on their land in Yorkshire, so it is fitting that the role of women in medieval society is included. There are biographies of the main players in the Templars' drama so that the reader can easily identify them and their part in the rise and fall of the Order.

The end of the Templars in Yorkshire came in 1312. After trials for heresy and other sins, the Order was suppressed by the Pope, and the Templars who admitted their errors were absolved and sent to repent in monasteries. Their story is held within these pages for modern readers to enjoy, along with information that will enable them to follow their footsteps through England's largest county.

Dr Evelyn Lord
University of Cambridge
Emeritus Fellow of Wolfson College

The Yorkshire Templars Organisation Chart

The Grand Master
The supreme head of the Knights Templar, answerable only to the Pope. He was based in Paris.

Master
There were eight Provincial Masters including one in England based in London. The others were in Aragon, Apulia, France, Hungary, Poitiers, Portugal and Scotland.

Preceptors
Areas owned by the Templars were administered from local preceptories (sometimes called commanderies). Preceptors headed up the preceptories.

The Preceptory of Yorkshire

The Templars' holdings in Yorkshire were so important that a 'chief' preceptor was appointed to oversee all the other preceptories in the county, each of which had its own preceptor.

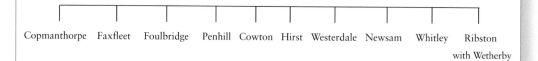

Copmanthorpe Faxfleet Foulbridge Penhill Cowton Hirst Westerdale Newsam Whitley Ribston with Wetherby

The post holders of Preceptor of the Preceptory of Yorkshire were:

Walter Brito, *c.* 1220
Roger de Scamelesbi, *c.* 1240
William de Merden, *c.* 1270
Robert de Haleghton, or Halton, occurs 1290, 1293
Thomas de Thoulouse, *c.* 1301
William de Grafton, *c.* 1304

1

A BRIEF HISTORY OF TEMPLAR ORIGINS

'The purpose of all war is peace'
Saint Augustine

'The Order of the Poor Knights of Christ of the Temple of Solomon in Jerusalem' was the full title of the enigma that became known simply as the Knights Templar. The first group of nine knights was offered part of the sacred Temple on the Mount to set up their quarters. This was a generous gesture on the part of King Baldwin II of Jerusalem, since it was within the walls of his own palace. The title 'Templar' was simply derived from the fact that their quarters were situated within the Temple at the Church of the Holy Sepulchre.

In time, the Knights Templar became superb builders, their castles and preceptories extended throughout the Holy Land. They had a hand in the rise of Gothic cathedrals in France and the round church became their trademark. The Order had knowledge of sacred geometry and intricate symbolism. The Templars touched almost every part of life: they were astute bankers, scribes, diplomats, administrators, negotiators, ship owners, war commanders, agricultural specialists; the list is endless. The legacy they left infiltrates all walks of our working life today. For instance, the credit card in its simplest form came about because the Templars introduced a promissory note, safeguarding huge sums of money both for pilgrims and kings.

The organisation of the Order followed a rigid formation, with the Grand Master at the head of the Order and regional Masters in various European countries; then the preceptor at the preceptories and their staff, which usually included chaplains and sergeants. In Yorkshire, all the preceptories came under the direction of York, though clearly the individual preceptors had a great deal of autonomy. A preceptory was a cross between a monastery and a manor. The Templars saw their main function as fulfilling their duty to God and spent time at prayer, just as any other religious order would have done. But they were also, essentially, lords of the manor and had to run that side of things effectively too. In order to run an efficient administration, they often employed people to carry out everyday functions for them.

Creation of the Knights Templar

There were three main Military Orders to begin with, each springing from passive origins. The Knights Hospitallers and the Teutonic Knights founded hospitals in the Middle East for pilgrims travelling from Europe to the holy city of Jerusalem. Until roughly the end of the eleventh century, the prevailing Muslims were happy to allow Christians to travel through the Middle East without duress to visit their holy place. However, in about 1095, Muslims from Turkey overran the Holy Land and from then pilgrims were no longer able to have safe passage. Many pilgrims were killed by the Muslims in their effort to visit Jerusalem. One very gruesome episode occurred at Eastertide in 1119 when a large number of pilgrims rested at an oasis and were set upon and killed by Muslim soldiers – not many lived to tell the tale. Now the journeys were not only arduous, but very dangerous as well. It was this event that led to the concept of the Knights Templar Order with their pledge to give safe passage to pilgrims. Hospitals became much in demand. In 1113, the Hospital of St John was recognised through a papal bull issued by Pope Paschal II to tend to the sick and weary pilgrim travellers.

In around 1127, the German hospital of St Mary in Jerusalem was founded and with it the embryonic beginning of the Teutonic Knights. Interestingly, in 1143, Pope Celestine II ordered the Knights Hospitallers to take over the management of the German hospital in Jerusalem, although he specified that it should maintain German roots and German speaking Brothers as German pilgrims did not speak French or understand Latin very well. After the loss of Jerusalem in 1187, another German hospital was founded around 1190 during the siege of Acre. This was the foundation of the Teutonic Order proper with Pope Celestine III recognising it in 1192 by granting the friars Augustine Rule.

The Templar Knights began in earnest with nine knights around 1119 in Jerusalem with a petition to King Baldwin of Jerusalem to offer protection to pilgrim travellers. The petition was granted and given the king's blessing; thus the potential for the Order had begun. In truth, the exact beginning of the possibilities for such an order took place much earlier in France; the origins of the idea of the Templar Knights can be traced back to about 1099.

There are a number of valid claims for this earlier date. The Knights Templar were the creative proposal of St Bernard of Clairvaux. He had the initiative and vision of combining a fighting force with spiritual devotion, thereby melding spiritual ethics and monastic principles into a disciplined army to establish a religious fighting force. Thus he created an order which had the seal of approval from Christ to fight for Christendom. This followed on from an edict by the charismatic Pope Urban II urging a crusade against the infidels on 'Christian' soil. At the Council of Clermont in 1095, Robert the Monk recorded Pope Urban's speech. Part of it demonstrates the emotive language used to persuade men to take arms, a translation reads:

> . . . that a race from the kingdom of the Persians, an accursed race, a race wholly alienated from God . . . violently invaded the lands of those Christians.

But if you are hindered by love of children, parents, or of a wife, remember what the Lord says in the Gospel, 'He that loveth father or mother more than me is not worthy of me'

Another of those present at the Council of Clermont, Fulcher of Chartres, reported this part of Urban's speech:

Let those who have formerly been accustomed to contend wickedly in private warfare against the faithful fight against the infidel, and bring to a victorious end the war which ought already to have been begun. Let those who have hitherto been robbers now become soldiers. Let those who have formerly contended against their brothers and relatives now fight against the barbarians as they ought. Let those who have formerly been mercenaries at low wages now gain eternal rewards. Let those who have been exhausting themselves to the detriment both of body and soul now strive for a twofold reward.

From this, it is easy to imagine the pressure brought to bear on men from all levels of society. Emotional blackmail was frequently used and as time went on, ever more calculated and cunning rhetoric was used to extort men to swell the ranks of the crusaders. Priests were the primary recruiters, resorting to parading celebrity knights and the singing of patriotic Christian hymns while encouraging men to join the Holy War. Thomas Aquinas trumpeted the justification of the crusades, declaring that performance equalled penance. In those days it was truly believed that people could be threatened by Divine judgement if they did not join a crusade. They believed they were engaged in acts of self-sanctification by joining them. It was stressed that they carried Christ's cloth on their shoulder and that they had Divine approval.

Apart from knights drawn from the upper echelons of society, lower ranks could become sergeants. Whether working in the stables or on the training field, all had hope of eternal redemption by joining the crusades and travelling to the Holy Land.

There were, however, pacifists and pessimists even in those days. There were also those who couldn't see the practicalities of a crusade and felt that war was not the way forward. Others were more concerned about the taxes which would have to be levied to pay for it all.

St Bernard was not only to bring his idea of a holy fighting force to fruition in the shape of the Knights Templar, but he also helped elevate their status to hitherto unprecedented heights. They became answerable only to the Pope above their sovereign king. They were the vassals of the Pope, carrying out many delicate negotiations, standing in his stead and gaining many privileges, much to the chagrin of various kings and chancellors.

Activities of the Order

Though the Knights Templar are commonly termed 'warrior monks', they were not a monastic order in the true sense. They did not live in a closed house, they did not have prayer times across twenty-four hours and their sole purpose was not the salvation of the soul of others, nor did they have an abbot at their head.

What they did do was take a vow of chastity, poverty and obedience. They assumed a rigorous lifestyle, giving up temptations of the flesh and giving personal property and wealth to the Knights Templar Order. They followed a conscientious order of prayer throughout the day beginning at 4 a.m. with Matins through to Vespers at 6 p.m. Compline would be said some time after the evening meal. Their food, though plain, was filling, with three meals a day.

Originally, the Order followed the Rule of St Augustine but this changed around 1130 through the authority of Bernard of Clairvaux. He was a Cistercian, and the Cistercians had formed from the Benedictines. There are marked resemblances between the two monastic orders. The rules were strict and retribution was exacted when rules were broken. Severe penalties included the confiscation of the mantle they wore under their cloaks, prison, or even expulsion from the Order.

The movement came to England and Scotland in the year 1128 when Hugues de Payens crossed the Channel, having solicited permission from Henry I to call men to arms to take the vows. This would lead to the formation of English and Scottish arms of the Order. De Payens also required financial assistance. It would be fair to say that he found England the more successful in swelling the ranks and coffers for the crusades' cause. By this time, the French Knights Templar had been actively supporting Alfonso I, King of Aragon (also known as the 'Battler') for some time. Alfonso won his greatest victories when he expelled the Moors from Zaragoza in 1118; he died during the siege of Fraga in 1134.

The first Temple round church was built about this time in Holborn, London, and the movement spread into Yorkshire roughly fourteen years later, with the first preceptory being founded somewhere between 1142 and 1185, probably at Cowton in North Yorkshire.

London became the administrative centre, but it was Yorkshire that possessed the broadest swath of English property. The London Temple focused on financial aims, while the Yorkshire preceptories were fixed on agricultural activities. The English arm of the Knights Templar gathered wealth for the Order through agricultural and financial industry and labour. It seems that the English Templar Order spent less time fighting in the East than their European counterparts, but raised riches in capital wealth for the Order as a whole.

Though the knights were from the cream of society, they wore plain unadorned garments; a white mantle with a red shoulder cross and a cloak also with a red shoulder cross. The Knights Templar became the cream of the fighting militia for Christ and the faith with a discipline second to none. They even earned the respect of the Saracens, the sworn enemies of Christians.

Pope Callistus II issued a bull in 1122 whereby the Templars became a 'lay religious community' and in time they were able to ordain their own priests, build their own churches and even have a hand in designing some of Europe's greatest cathedrals.

Despite the motivation behind the Knights Templar inception – to provide safe passage for travellers, particularly pilgrims journeying through the Holy Land – it

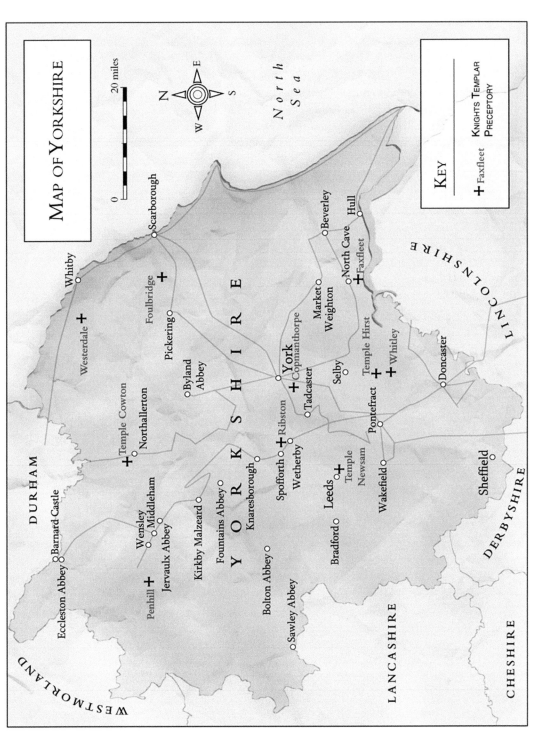

Map of Yorkshire showing Knights Templar preceptories. (Jonathan Young)

was not the main reason for their continued existence. As a disciplined fighting force, their military might overtook their original protective origins. The Templar Knights were to become efficient and fearsome soldiers, landowners with vast amounts of property, practiced farmers, skilled sailors, learned men and eventually, accomplished bankers. This last endeavour was largely to bring about their downfall.

Many legends have sprung up around the Knights Templar, and as Karen Ralls writes in her foreword to the book *The Templar Papers* by Oddvar Olsen: 'even during the time of the Knights Templar 1119–1312 "history" and "myths" were already entwined.'

2

TEMPLE COWTON

(near Northallerton, c. 1142)

Around AD 80, the Romans built a road, known as Dere Street. It was 180 miles long and stretched from York to the Firth of Forth in Scotland. Parts of it still exist, with both the A1(M) and the A68 overlaying it in places. The Templars would have found it just as useful as the Romans did all those centuries before and for the same reason: it gave them easy access to their possessions in Scotland. This probably explains why, in 1142, they built a preceptory near Dere Street in the vicinity of the village of East Cowton.

This area now consists of quiet, winding country lanes, high hedges and mile upon mile of arable farmland. In the far distance, hills can be seen where the remains of the distant Penhill Preceptory chapel lie quietly among the grazing cows. There's nothing which can be seen of the modern East Cowton's Templar preceptory now; in fact, nobody is quite sure exactly where it stood. However, an association remains with the name of Temple House Farm near the village itself. The name 'Cowton' is Anglo-Saxon in origin and dairy farms in the area still reflect that early meaning of 'cow farm'. Nearby North Cowton goes a step further, with several houses having 'byre', meaning cowshed, in their names.

The preceptory

Founded in 1142, Temple Cowton was probably the first preceptory to be established in Yorkshire and was certainly very important to the Order. This is underlined by the fact that at the time of their suppression, when all the Order's possessions were being scrutinised, a chest was found at Temple Cowton which contained all the charters which related to their estates in Yorkshire; documents concerning their various estates in the rest of England and Scotland were also discovered. It seems that these chests, along with one found at Faxfleet, disappeared on their way from Yorkshire to London at the time of the Order's suppression.

The preceptory's importance is further demonstrated by the fact that Edward I stayed there in 1300 on one of his many journeys to Scotland. William Wallace had started a rebellion in Scotland in 1297 and was a thorn in the English king's side until his capture on 5 August 1305. Temple Cowton proved a useful staging post at which to leave provisions for Edward's frequent sorties north of the border.

Temple Cowton, like Penhill, benefited from the generosity of a benefactor, Roger de Mowbray, who, around 1142, granted them timber from his forests at Nidderdale, Masham and Malzeard. By the time of the Order's suppression in 1308, it is reported that the buildings included a hall, chamber, chapel, kitchen, brewhouse and smithy. Sadly, none of them remain to be seen.

Battle of the Standard

Four years before any of this was built, the Battle of the Standard (also known as the Battle of Northallerton), was fought nearby, just two miles north of Northallerton near the village of Brompton. Although this battle is sometimes referred to as the Battle of Cowton Moor, we know from a contemporary account that it actually took place some eight miles from there. The confusion may have arisen due to additions made to a contemporary text a considerable time after it had been written.

The Battle of the Standard was so called because some members of the English Army had brought a frame along with them, in the middle of which they stood a very tall ship's mast which they called the Standard. It had nothing at all to do with flags, although the banners of St Wilfred and St John were displayed at the battle.

While on the subject of banners, Edward I paid one of the monks from Beverley 8 pennies a day for carrying his banner of St John while he was with the King's Army. He was also paid a penny a day to take it back to the monastery.

The background to the Battle of the Standard is that in July 1138, King David I of Scotland made his third incursion into England that year. He came on the pretext of acting in the interests of his niece, Matilda, who was contesting the right to the English throne with King Stephen. It is thought that his real intention was to take possession of Northumberland. Whichever it was, David chose his moment carefully, taking advantage of the fact that Stephen was down near Bristol trying to deal with his barons' revolt.

Archbishop Thurston of York, the King's Lieutenant in the north, successfully raised an army and presented the mission of repelling the Scots as akin to a Holy Crusade. His army marched from York to Thirsk from where two barons went on to negotiate with David, but were unsuccessful. The Scottish Army crossed into Yorkshire on 21 August and began ravaging the county. The English moved to intercept them.

It is directly due to Archbishop Thurston's successful recruitment drive that we know so much about the Battle of the Standard. Because there was such an important person within the Church involved, contemporary ecclesiastical chroniclers fell over themselves to record events.

Where there is now agricultural land, the two armies faced each other – the Scots on a hill to the north, the English on a hill 600yds south of them, blocking their advance. The fight took place on what both Richard of Hexham and Ailred of Rievaulx described as a 'plain'. This is understood at that time to have meant an expanse of uncultivated moorland. The area had suffered under William the Conqueror's 'harrying of the north', so it is likely that this land had not yet been returned to cultivation.

The Scots had superiority in terms of numbers, although the exact size of both armies is uncertain. The Scottish attack was led by unarmoured infantry – at their insistence – ahead of knights clad in protective armour. English bowmen unleashed their arrows and cut the enemy's infantry to pieces. Those Scots who did manage to make it through to the English lines were slaughtered in hand to hand fighting against the well-armed local army. It didn't all go England's way, but after two hours, they forced the Scottish army into a retreat which turned into a rout. For some reason, the English did not follow to carry out mopping up operations.

Military training, weapons & armour

Nearly 150 years later, the whole business of training an English army became much more organised. During the reign of King Edward I, the Statute of Winchester of 1285 came into being. The statute made it compulsory for every male over the age of fifteen to own a weapon. The weapon would vary according to status. The least in status and, by definition, the most prolific, was the bow and arrow. Good archers could earn many special privileges and practice was thoroughly encouraged. Henry I went as far as to grant that, should an archer practising his craft accidentally kill another, then it should not be held against him as a crime.

Later, King Edward III, a highly successful military leader, complained that the people followed useless and dishonest games like stone throwing and cock fighting. Thus, he ordered the population to practise with their bows and arrows on feast days, as well as at other allocated times. Indeed, the Statute of Cambridge ordered all young men to give up the playing of dice, quoits, skittles and the like and to take part in archery practice instead!

Every town and village had to set up 'butts' which were for target practice. Practice was usually led by an old soldier, a bowman who was paid a small fee for the job. Medieval archers were one of the most efficient fighting forces of their time. For hundreds of years, they were, if correctly deployed, seen as the 'make or break' in the outcome of a battle. They had quick-fire ability and could bring a battle to a winning conclusion, even when the odds were against them. English bowmen were particularly good in the field with the rapid fire technique as they preferred the longbow to the crossbow. Until about the end of the twelfth century, the longbow was an uncomplicated affair, with the arrow head normally barbed.

As battles became more protracted, and when sieges became quite prolonged and protection in the Holy Land often meant defence of strongholds and narrow defiles, the bowmen became an ever more important arm of the overall defence and attack weapon of medieval battles. The best English bows were made from the yew tree. The pale sapwood resisted stretching and the darker heartwood resisted compression, thereby giving it a natural spring action. Though yew was the best wood for the bow, it did not have enough strength to withstand the 'string' cutting into the wood; therefore, horn tips or nocks were inserted into the ends of the bow for protection.

Equally respected were the bow makers. A skilled bow maker would be in high demand, as his selection of the wood and his skill in producing the bow were of paramount importance. An arrow when loosed from the bow does not travel in a straight line, it arcs in flight. Thus, the archer needed to be able to judge distances and have an understanding of angles as well being reliant on the bow maker to have produced a true bow.

There were, of course, crossbowmen, but these tended to be more popular on the Continent than in England. Widely used in Norman Europe, the crossbow was a truly brutal weapon and in 1139 the Church banned its use. However, this did not prevent the champions of the weapon using it and it appears that the decree was quietly forgotten.

Crossbowmen were sometimes mounted; a measure of affluence was necessary in order to own a horse. During battles, mounted crossbowmen clearly had an advantage over mounted soldiers carrying a spear or lance.

The ingredient of victory for the English was quite simply the rapid fire of the longbow over the crossbow, as can be attested in the history of the fourteenth century. The worst thing for an English bowman was to be caught and have his two 'bow fingers' cut off. This is where the habit of putting up two fingers is supposed to have originated.

The Bayeux Tapestry shows that the javelin was widely used both by the French and English, but it seems that by the twelfth century, it had all but been abandoned except by the Spanish who seem to have retained it as a favourite weapon.

Boys of nobility had swords and would most probably have had the use of a sword long before the age of fifteen. Alfonso, the third son of Edward I, is known to have had a little castle with siege weapons with which to practise, as did his younger brother, later to become Edward II.

The knights were at their most powerful as a fighting force in the medieval period. Their weapons were a sword, lance and sometimes a mace. In close battles, some knights preferred a mace to a sword. It is easy to understand why – all the weight was focused in the head of the mace, the head being made from flanges welded to a hollow shaft. Therefore, when the mace was hefted onto the foe, the resultant blow was devastating.

In the hands of the formidable and disciplined Templars, these weapons were put to terrifying use. However, the sword was the weapon the knights greatly preferred; a straight double-edged blade with a wicked flat point. The sword handle was often decorated, sometimes with precious stones, though the Templars' swords would not have been so decorated. Their swords were often finely etched, as many swords were. The shield part of the sword was almost always flat at this time; indeed as far back as the time of the Norman invasion, the Bayeux Tapestry shows soldiers balancing their cups and plates on the flat shield of their swords. Later in the twelfth century, triangular shaped shields became popular.

By the thirteenth century, the sword underwent an adjustment which allowed the sword to penetrate the knights' armour, as the development was towards a more acute point to allow for a thrusting, rather than a cutting movement.

Having hefted a sword from the fourteenth century, I was amazed at how light it was – about 5lbs. I felt that with practice, even I could have used it. (I can also now accept that Joan of Arc would have been able to use a sword with great ability!) The earlier, broader shaped sword would only have been a little heavier, so

Examples of medieval swords.

a grown man or knight would certainly have been lethal using his sword.

Spurs, or to be more accurate, pick spurs were a must for a knight. Developed during the time of the Romans, spurs were worn on the heels. Unhappily, they were used to provoke the horses forward during battle. They were used throughout the medieval period and were often decorated with silver and gold foil. They became symbols of knighthood and a new knight was said to have 'won his spurs' when he became a soldier of Christ.

Some of the Great Seals give an insight into various modes of armour, for kings and the high-born at least. The Great Seal of King Henry II shows the king astride an unarmoured horse. The chain-mail armour is still very similar to that worn by the Norman knights of the late eleventh century. Henry wears a mail shirt and leg defences. The helmet is conical in shape and has a nose bar of a type that continued, in some quarters, into the thirteenth century. The Great Seal of King Richard I shows a flat helmet fitted with a face guard. The mail shirt is still worn, but chain mittens are an addition worn to protect the hands. The sword is also shown, a cross hilted design used for cutting often seen in medieval art. The Great Seal of King Henry III shows a fully enclosed helmet, which by now was becoming increasingly popular. He is also wearing a thick padded surcoat which reaches down to his mid-calf. The Great Seal of Edward I shows a change in the design of the shield. Here the design is smaller and convex as there was now less of a need to protect the head. Also, the horse now had some protective covering, an outer housing over some kind of chain-mail or armour.

Siege engines were a significant part of medieval warfare. If a castle was to be taken, then these had to be used, whereby huge stones were 'slung' to batter the thick walls of a castle. However, siege engines had to be used in conjunction with other battle apparatus to be really effective, which included battering rams, together with the practice of undermining and tunnelling beneath castle walls. This caused structures to become insecure, leading to the walls being unable to withstand the assault by the siege engine.

For the defenders of a castle, their recourse was somewhat restricted. Both the crossbowmen and the longbowmen were indispensable in keeping would-be attackers from scaling the walls. Heavy stones would be aimed at the attackers, smashing many of them at once. Another ploy was 'Greek fire' – an explosive, nasty combination of oil and other ingredients. Fire arrows were also employed by both attackers and defenders.

A Templar effigy

A good example of what a Templar era knight looked like can be seen in the beautiful Norman church of St Mary at Kirkby Fleetham. It is alleged that this is an effigy of Sir Nicholas Stapleton who was a Knight Templar and belonged either to the preceptory at Temple Cowton or the one at Temple Hirst. Although a Templar would not have ordered such an effigy to be made, there is more to this particular story. Sir Nicholas was the eldest son of Sir Roger Stapleton, a judge and Lord of the Manor of Kirkby Fleetham, and Sir Nicholas predeceased his father, who later died in 1290. It is thought that Sir Roger's second son, Miles, ordered this effigy to

St Mary's Church, Kirkby Fleetham, which houses the effigy of Sir Nicholas Stapleton.

Effigy of Sir Nicholas Stapleton.

be made in memory of his Knight Templar brother. The effigy lies in a recess just before the altar rail and contains delightful detail. The figure is wearing chain-mail that covers him from head to hips, over which there is a long linen surcoat. A small belt encircles the waist and there's a thin band round his head just above forehead level. He's carrying a pointed shield which bears the Stapleton coat of arms and a small stylized lion sits at his feet looking at him. The effigy is in excellent condition and gives a good insight into what knights wore in the late thirteenth century.

The clothing the Knights Templar could wear was governed by their Rules. The knights wore a white cloak and the sergeants a black one. Their distinctive red cross was added by Pope Eugenius in 1146. It was stipulated that the robes should be without finery or fur. Those who received new robes had to return their old ones so that they could be passed on to the squires and sergeants or given to the poor. Who got what was decided by the draper, who was in charge of distributing all the Templars' clothing. They were allowed to wear linen shirts if they wanted to, in recognition of the intense heat they might experience in the Holy Land. However, pointed shoes and shoelaces were out of the question. They were 'abominable things' and belonged to pagans, not Christians. Finally, they were not permitted to wear their hair or clothes too long.

Templar tenants

If Sir Nicholas was a member of Temple Cowton, he would have been familiar with its tenants. The 1185 inquest records them as follows:

> Near Cowton they have 6 carrucates of the gift of Robert Chambard of which
> 4 are in demesne and 2 are assized by these men.
> Ralph Tait 1 bovate for a rent of 5 shillings and 2 hens, 20 eggs and
> 4 boonworks.
> Geoffrey, his son, 1 bovate for a rent of 5 shillings and aforesaid services.
> Reginald 1 toft and 2 acres for 20 pennies and aforesaid services.
> Also the same Reginald 1 toft and 2 acres for 20 pennies and aforesaid
> services.
> Torold 1 toft and 2 acres for 20 pennies.
> Ralph, merchant, 1 toft for 12 pennies and aforesaid services.
> Hernisius 1 toft for 12 pennies and aforesaid services.
> Adam, miller, 1 toft and 2 acres for 20 pennies and aforesaid services.
> Adelhard 1 toft for twelve pennies and aforesaid services.
> William, smith, 1 toft for 12 pennies and aforesaid services.
> Alexander 1 toft for 12 pennies and aforesaid services.
> Of the gift of William Daudrey and William of Cowton, William the savage
> 1 toft for 12 pennies and aforesaid services.
> In the other Cowton [i.e. South Cowton, which no longer exists] Eda, widow,
> 3 acres for 2 shillings and aforesaid services.
> Ernald 1 toft for 12 pennies and aforesaid services.
> Richard, cheesemonger, 6 acres for 2 shillings and aforesaid services.
> Hucca 1 toft for 12 pennies and aforesaid services.
> William Le Wake 1 toft for 12 pennies and aforesaid services.
> Henry 2 tofts and 6 acres for 30 pennies and aforesaid services.
> Also 2 bovates of the aforesaid donor which are in demesne.
> By the brothers purchase from Ralph, son of Gude, 2 acres which are in
> demesne.

As at Temple Newsam (*see* Chapter 5), the Templars bought land, as well as it being gifted to them. Within the Inquest a few other properties are mentioned which may well have belonged to Temple Cowton, but could also have belonged to another preceptory.

Among the tenants listed above, there are three which are of particular interest. Did the mill where Adam the miller worked belong to the Templars? Did William the smith work in the preceptory's smithy? Most intriguing of all, why was William referred to as 'the savage' and where did he come from?

3

PENHILL

(near Leyburn, c. 1142)

The preceptory

As one leaves the rugged limestone cliffs of upper Wensleydale behind, the craggy, ridged countryside begins to moderate a little; the grasses cling thicker and soften the rough edges of the cliffs. The approach to the village of Swithinwaite in lower Wensleydale follows a long winding hill, leading to a plateau of arable farm land. From here, to find the remains of Penhill Preceptory chapel one has to climb yet again. A rough path of huge chunks of limestone which follows a water course climbs up to another narrow plateau where the Templar chapel is located. That the remains have been preserved is due to The National Monuments Act 1913–53. The site is fairly typical of the Yorkshire Templar preceptories inasmuch as it commands an advantageous view. From the high ground, miles of countryside can be surveyed. To the north and west is an escarpment, which takes the eye to Penhill itself. It is distinct and unmistakable in shape, dominating wherever one looks in this part of Wensleydale. There is considerable scrub and thickets of trees surrounding the narrow strip of meadowland where the chapel stands, but this scrub is relatively young; 700 years ago the view would have been uninhibited.

It is interesting that Wensleydale was not the original name of the dale; it was called Yoredale or Uredale after the steam that runs through it. Almost all dales are named after the stream or river that flow through them; however, there is always an exception to the rule and Wensleydale is it, being named after the village instead. The name change came some time before the end of the eighteenth century. It seems that the market town of Wensley was rather important until at least the sixteenth century. As it lies at the head of the valley, it would have been a focal point for local markets. The river that runs through Wensleydale is shown on modern maps as the River Ure. The famous abbey of Jervaulx was also known originally as Yore-valley Abbey before becoming the French sounding Jervaulx.

The chapel

The chapel was dedicated to Our Lady and to St Catherine. It would have been joined to, or at least very close to, other residential buildings, such as a dormitory, kitchen, etc. – none of which have been excavated. However, the uneven surface in the field around the chapel ruins suggests there is much more to be found. The remains of the chapel were uncovered in 1840 and consist of four 3ft high stone walls about 4½ft thick, with a space in the south wall that may have been a doorway. It is over 50ft long from east to west and about 19ft wide. The chancel contains the stone base of an altar, but the altar itself has not been found. Three empty stone coffins and their cover slabs lie in the centre of the main area. There were human remains in the coffins when they were originally found, but these have long since disappeared. This is a very peaceful site, with cows grazing quietly nearby – and on occasion, inside the chapel itself!

There were actually two preceptories built here. The first mention of a preceptory at Penhill was around 1170–81, although timber for buildings had been donated some years before by Roger de Mowbray from his nearby forests at Nidderdale and Masham as well as from Malzeard. The first site comprises the earthwork remains of a courtyard which was surrounded by buildings, with a second courtyard on a higher terrace. Another 65sq. ft earthwork is thought to be the footings for a tower, which was a common feature of all Templar preceptories. The second preceptory, which lies to the south of the original one and contains the excavated chapel, follows a similar pattern. The courtyard is to the south-east of the chapel and the

Penhill chapel looking towards the altar.

Penhill chapel altar base and stone coffins.

Penhill chapel showing the thickness of the wall.

*Penhill chapel
stone coffins.*

earthworks indicate further buildings. There was also a mill, mill ponds and water channels to the west of the chapel.

The excavation of the chapel seems to have taken place in 1840, but there appears to have been another dig between January 1880 and December 1889. Records at the Archaeological Data Service state: 'Excavated by the proprietor of Swinethwaite Hall; the finds, however, were not located there; their whereabouts is unknown'.

On the eastern edge of the Pennines and the North Yorkshire Moors, extensive forest clearing took place long before our Templar timeline. However, the Penhill Preceptory Templars would have cleared their land of scrub. Plants such as sorrel only prosper after trees have been cleared as more light reaches the ground and other plant forms can take a foothold. Cleared areas provided space for crops, cattle, sheep and pigs. The open space allowed new grasses to grow for cattle feed. The felled trees were used for construction and for making a whole host of tools.

Wood was also used widely for smelting purposes. Thickets of trees were left as a food source for their nuts and berries and for medicinal uses and dyes.

New trade routes and the related ship building, immigration and food demand brought in by different cultures meant that the burgeoning population required more land to be cleared. All of the above helped to put pressure on the land and as urbanisation grew, so did deforestation. The Templars played their part in the boon of food demand. They usually had a number of farms attached to their preceptories from which they drew both rent and food and, as previously mentioned, they cleared hitherto uncultivated land to use both for living and food production.

England, in common with the rest of Europe, experienced an expansion in economic activity. Forests and their many riches were part of that upsurge and indeed, formed the foundation for the enrichment of medieval society. The high point of deforestation occurred between 1100 and 1350. The ecclesiastical and lay orders 'cleared and built' with the cry 'to the Glory of God' while piety and devoutness often went hand in hand with personal gain.

By the end of the twelfth century, the decline of forests led to the aristocracy putting further restraints on deforestation by having tighter controls on the forests used for hunting. The rights and customs that grew from these measures demonstrated how serious the problem had become. These new measures were not welcomed by the peasants, though in reality, there was little they could do about it. History shows that, to a degree, we must give thanks to those nobles for the fact that we still have a few ancient forests, however hard it was on the peasants of the time. There are now organisations that look after what remaining woodlands we have, although their measures are not as draconian as those far off nobles. They will undoubtedly have the thanks of future generations.

Agricultural technology & horses

By this time, the crop rotation system was changing from that of two fields, one with crops of one sort or another and one which was fallow. Instead, this was beginning to be replaced with three fields in use. This was partly due to natural fertilizer being garnered from spent crops such as legumes and it being used more efficiently. Partly, it was due to the development of the three-wheeled plough with the added ability of the shod horse over oxen; the horse was more effective and productive in using the plough. There are some authorities, however, who maintain that there was very little in the way of improved agricultural technology during medieval times. They argue that the big changes did not occur until the sixteenth century. Certainly the fourteenth-century Luttrell Psalter has illustrations showing a team of four oxen pulling what looks like a mould-board plough. On the following page a horse is shown pulling a harrow. So unquestionably, both animals were still being used in farming at that time.

Nonetheless, horses were a vital component of medieval life. Apart from pulling harrows and ploughs on farms, where they could sometimes find themselves harnessed alongside an ox, they could also be used to turn wheels in corn mills.

The end product was then transported to market, again using horse power. Horses were invaluable to medieval economics, being used to transport raw materials and finished goods, farm produce, building materials and people from place to place. They were also used in battle.

Some accounts of Penhill refer to the discovery of spurs, horseshoes and fragments of armour and conclude that this is evidence that a cavalry training facility existed here. We could not locate a record of these finds, but it may simply be that such a record is now in private hands. The assumption that Penhill Preceptory was used for training cavalry is easy to understand because of the area's connection with horses. Just down the road near Leyburn there is a cluster of over a dozen racehorse training stables; indeed, Yorkshire is renowned for an abundance of these establishments. However, this connection is comparatively recent. Isaac Cape, a jockey and the first specialist racehorse trainer in the area, didn't arrive until 1733 and the area's racehorse training industry began with him. But there is another equine connection. Just a couple of miles away as the crow flies stands Jervaulx Abbey, a place renowned for its horse-breeding expertise from the time the Templars occupied Penhill until the Dissolution activities of Henry VIII.

At this time in history, horses were referred to by their type or purpose, rather than by breed. They could also be referred to by where they came from, or even by the name of the breeder. So it's interesting to speculate whether the monks' horses were referred to as Jervaulxes, Yorevalleys, Cistercians or something else altogether. One of the most important horse breeding centres to supply the Order with the mounts it needed in the East was at Richerenches in France, the headquarters of the Knights Templar in Provence. This would have been handy for the Templars' embarkation ports along France's Mediterranean coast.

Edward I was known to use Templar preceptories in the north as staging posts for his battles in Scotland. So were the spurs, horseshoes and fragments of armour really indicative of a cavalry training post – or were they simply evidence of Edward's soldiers travelling between preceptories making deliveries? Horse harness adornments with the Templar cross on them have been found at Fridaythorpe and Goodmanham in East Yorkshire, and also between Escrick and Naburn near York. Perhaps these belonged to members of the Order on the move around Yorkshire.

On his travels around Yorkshire, a Templar may have ridden a rouncy. Templars stationed in the Middle East would have ridden this type of horse on their way to battle, saving their warhorse for when it was needed most. Some authorities maintain that a rouncy was not a riding horse at all, but rather was used as a pack animal. Another mount for everday use was the palfrey, its short legs and long body rendering a comfortable, gentle, ambling gait. So the Knights Templar may have used palfreys to travel round at home and abroad. Women riders would have ridden astride their mounts, as the side-saddle had yet to be invented.

When it comes to war horses (destriers) historians seem unable to agree on just how big they were. One school of thought talks about horses almost the size of today's Shire horses, another says that they were smaller, lighter and faster. Both arguments are based on the weight of the armour worn by the knights, which

Horse harness adornment found at Barmby Moor, East Yorkshire. (Courtesy of I. Szymanski)

Horse harness adornments found at Fridaythorpe, East Yorkshire. (Courtesy of I. Szymanski)

Horse harness adornments found at Leavening, south of Malton, North Yorkshire. (Courtesy of I. Szymanski)

weighed in the region of 50–100lbs. A point put forward by those who favour the Shire-type horses is that the animal's weight was used to advantage during battle to put as much force as possible behind the thrust of a lance or sword. Others say it was the weight of the rider that governed the power of the thrust and that lighter horses could easily manage the weight of the armour and, most importantly, had the agility needed in a fight.

There was a Templar Rule which allowed difficult mounts to be returned to the 'caravanne' and an appeal to be made to the marshal for a replacement, although Templars were not allowed to request specific horses. A brother was not, according to the Rule, expected to put up with a horse that stopped suddenly, refused to move or threw its rider. Templar horses, and indeed those of other combatants, were known to bite and kick each other, as well as anyone who happened to be in range. Among other things, the marshal supervised the allocation of mounts and took care of animals sent to him from Europe.

Pilgrimage & religious donations

The chapel at Penhill demonstrates once again how important the spiritual aspect of life was for the Templars. Such spirituality was also strong with many lay people as well as the various ecclesiastical orders and as such, pilgrimage was common among all walks of life. As we know from the Chaucer tales, even for the criminal it held the possibility of freedom. It was the high point in life to accomplish a pilgrimage in medieval Europe and no less so in England.

If an illness invaded a household and all conventional doctors, healing women and non-conventional healing had failed, then to turn to a pilgrimage would be the last but best hope for cure. The pilgrimage journey was deeply embedded in the medieval psyche. There were myriad reasons to go on pilgrimage and as many places to journey to. In England, Walsingham and Canterbury were just two. Further afield, eleventh-century Cluniac monks had made St James' shrine at Santiago de Compostella a famous place for pilgrims to visit; other sites were visited on the way, such as Toulouse and St Sernin or Chartres, with worship made to the Virgin Mary. Rome was, of course, the top site in Europe; it was, though, a perilous expedition. The given route from England was by way of Flanders, Antwerp, Coblenz, and Ulm, through the Alps, on to Verona, Bologna and Siena, and so to Rome. It was, and still is, a very long, gruelling and demanding journey by any standards. The route was well colonised though, with plenty of inns and hamlets along the way, with people always willing to give a bed to a pilgrim.

For the holy and devout, the Holy Land was the place to go. These journeys were always fraught with danger of one sort or another. For the Holy Land a pilgrim first needed to travel to Venice where the majority of pilgrim ships left during May. There was the possibility of capture by pirates, storms, poor food and very cramped conditions. Pilgrimage had become, by the eleventh century, a thriving and organised throng of people travelling thousands of miles in all directions across Europe and the Middle East.

One William Wey wrote a journal to help other pilgrims plan their journeys to the Holy Land. His advice included paying for the return journey as well as the outward, and ensuring that the deal was signed in the presence of a member of the judiciary. He also recommended the plucky traveller purchase a mattress for the sea journey and to be sure to take a place on the top deck rather than in the bowels of the ship. By the late Middle Ages, French had overtaken Latin as the language of conversation and several 'conversation manuals' were written to help travellers.

Although Western Europeans did not deliberately set out to explore the world until the fifteenth century, their Christian beliefs had infiltrated the world at large. Christianity became lawful around AD 313 which ended 300 years of persecution. There were many different sects, but by the fourth century the Catholic Church was dominant. The Roman Emperor Theodosius I made the Catholic religion the official one of the empire by *c*. AD 700. By that time, smaller sects had withered away. By the medieval period, most churches could trace their ancestry back to the Catholic Church. Medieval Christianity was profoundly influenced by monasticism, a practice that had proliferated from fourth-century Egypt. Eventually, the founding of both the Dominican and the Franciscan Order of Friars altered the spiritual life of the Church. Their members took on pastoral care in the community while maintaining their vows, as opposed to cloistered orders. The new orders sought to encourage devotion to God through their daily work and to see God in all that they did throughout the day. In other words, one could see holiness and goodness outside the Church and closed orders.

The Catholic religion had disseminated across the continents through, among other reasons, invaders attacking Europe. These were the Vikings in the North, the Magyarsin in the East and the Muslims of North Africa in the South. The Vikings took Catholicism to Iceland and Greenland. The Magyarsin, together with other central Europeans, were converted by *c*. AD 1000. Sicily and the Balearics were recaptured from the Muslims in a number of wars supported by the papacy from around the eleventh century. These spasmodic wars did not really end until Granada fell to the Catholic kings of Spain in 1492. Christianity had certainly spread to the Middle East, and the Church had developed differently there. In the early days, the Catholic Church and the Byzantine Church were unified in the business of faith. However, political tensions were straining the two cultures. The crunch came with the sacking of Constantinople by the Fourth Crusade in 1204. This act aggravated the problems and later the rupture was complete and has yet to be healed.

A Christian centre grew up in Antioch from which emerged some excessive forms of devotion. For instance, St Symeon Stylites left his monastery and spent the remainder of his life, some twenty odd years, staying on top of ever higher columns. The last one was said to be over 60ft tall. Huge numbers of people sought him out to seek intercession from him for their illnesses. One can only assume that they gathered at the base of his column and shouted up to him!

When the followers of the prophet Mohammad conquered Syria and Palestine, they allowed all forms of Christianity, provided they did not try to convert Muslims; within 300 years, there was a huge conversion to Islam. The First Crusade of 1096 brought much of the lands under Western rule for almost as long as the Islamic conversions took, over 200 years. During this time the Maronite Church flourished;

it had it own ranking and Canon Law, but it came under the jurisdiction of the Pope and the alliance continues to this day. Though the Westerners were driven out in 1291, the Franciscan Order created a base from which they could attend to the weary pilgrims and around 1336, the Catholic Church also reasserted itself.

The Catholic Church always patronised the arts; Romanesque and Gothic churches were well-endowed with frescoes, stained glass, marble, statues and all manor of *objets d'art*. Wherever Rome held influence, Gothic art flourished; it stood as a reassertion of the established Church after a serious decline and of Rome emerging supreme over the Holy German Empire which had caused a rupture within Catholicism. Monastic orders helped to fire a new wave of religious revival and also had an influence on twelfth-century art.

People from all walks of life left money to the Church, usually a specific one rather than to the Catholic Church in general, with precise instructions for its use. This practice still occurs to this day. For example, in western Spain, thirteen miles from the ancient city of Salamanca, a 'new basilica' is being built in the birthplace of St Theresa and dedicated to her. The building of the basilica has been ongoing for around a hundred years. A current canon, whose responsibility it is to oversee the building, has full coffers due to money being given for specific devotional works and for the glorification of the interior of the church, such as for the decoration of the columns, the altar or the pulpit. However, he does not have enough money to pay for the roof to be completed, so the interior decoration of the church cannot begin. The gardens surrounding the church are beautiful with mature shrubs and trees, as no doubt money for this project was donated very early on!

Incidentally, during the building of the old cathedral of Salamanca built during the Templar timeline in the eleventh century (as opposed to the 'new' sixteenth-century cathedral), a building tax dispensation was given by the king, the amount of which depended at the time on the construction costs as a whole; 700 years later, the tax dispensation is still applicable to the new basilica.

Often, the act of a dedicated donation was in part to ensure a smooth passage to the afterlife. Later, the fashion of including the 'donor' in paintings would prevail.

In the Eastern provinces, church art developed in different ways. No other society has approached the quantity or quality of technical expertise which the Byzantines accomplished in the sphere of mosaics, a specialist and aristocratic form of art. Though not exclusive to religious art, mosaics offered a form of art in which the viewer could engage and be reminded of the stories from the Bible in the same way that frescoes did in the Western churches.

Education

The ecclesiastical world had held guardianship over learning and education. The secular world of kings and government relied on them to draft laws and hold records. The Templar Order became adroit at cornering this market in many ways. Though justices, sheriffs and the like depended on the clergy, the Templars worked with the upper echelons of society. However, by the twelfth century, universities and the blooming of 'an intellectual strata' in society reduced their grip on education to a minimum.

There is no real evidence about education for the masses in the medieval era. What education there was varied enormously, but was often limited to reading, singing and religious teachings. Many clergy thought that women would misuse any education they had. However, the main obstacle to education for boys or girls was a question of finance. Education was expensive, particularly in terms of books because vellum was costly, so much of education was a matter of word of mouth. Indeed, English universities of the time often consisted simply of a group of students standing on a street corner, gathered around their tutor to listen to what he had to say. Just as they do today, students went off to study abroad, but in 1167 Henry II banned English students from attending the prestigious University of Paris, which led to the rapid expansion of Oxford University. With medieval universities on the rise, many households were able to employ students as tutors for their male children.

Education flourished much more for men than women. In around 1225, Thomas of Aquinas, a renowned Italian priest and teacher of the time, stated the then widely held belief that: 'Woman is subject to man on account of the weakness of her nature . . . man is the beginning of woman and her end, just as God is the beginning and end of every creature. Children ought to love their father more than they love their mother.'

The subject of education for women was a hotly debated issue for many, many decades. Medieval society as a whole, but in particular the authoritative domains of the Church, really had no place for educated women. However, Vincent of Beauvais, writing in 1254, recommended wealthy parents to allow their daughters to learn to read and write 'in order that they be kept busy and thereby escape harmful thoughts and pleasures of the flesh'. For girls wishing to become nuns, learning to read and write was part of their training. Some studied Latin, but for the vast majority of girls, marriage and motherhood were the most they could hope for. One exception was Christine of Pizan, born in the twelfth century. Christine was given an education far beyond that of most noblewomen, or men for that matter; her father was a scholar and astrologer and clearly forward thinking for the time. She later earned her living as a writer and debated with leading clerics of the day on the rights of women – perhaps one of the first women with feminist views!

Many men, however, had education as a matter of course, at least in the circles of the nobility, but all knights were not, by any means, well educated. It was the tradition for noble families to send their young male children to begin training as a knight at about the age of seven. The child would be sent to the house of another noble for instruction and preparation. Education, in terms of reading and writing, was generally thought not to be necessary, though many did learn these skills if their tuition included a tutor from the clergy. However, we know that many Templars were learned men.

Templar tenants

The 1185 Inquest, a countrywide survey of Templar holdings, presents something of a problem when it comes to discerning which tenancies were administered from Penhill Preceptory. There is only one unambiguous reference which says:

'Near Penhill they have 2 carrucates of land of the gift of William, son of Hervey, which they have in demesne'. But a little later in the document there is a whole raft of tenancies which are described as being 'towards the North by York'. This discrepancy has entailed sitting with the Inquest details in one hand and a map in the other, trying to make an intelligent guess as to which preceptory 'towards the North by York' took care of which tenants. Therefore, the list of tenants below are more of a possibility than a certainty. The preceptories involved are Penhill, Temple Cowton, Westerdale and Foulbridge. Some of the entries illustrate that it wasn't only the influential noblemen who made donations of this nature to the Templars:

> Near Leyburn of the gift of Michael 1 toft and 1 acre which Thomas holds for 12 pennies and all services.
> Also of the gift of Michael 1 toft for 12 pennies which Roger holds.
> In Aldfield of the gift of Ralph, son of Aldrid, 2 acres which Baldwin holds for 12 pennies for all services.
> In (Thornton) Watlass 2 acres of the gift of Hervey which Ailward holds for 12 pennies for all services.
> Near Burril of the gift of William, son of Jordan, 2 tofts which Robert holds for 12 pennies for all services.

Children's games & toys

It is often thought that in the medieval period, children had rather a hard time and did not indulge in games. However, this is, in many cases, a misconception; children had many games, some of which would be recognised today. Rattles existed for babies and toddlers, not only did they exist, but the ability to buy a rattle indicates that there was mass production. Manufactured rattles have been found, though predominately in London. While bought toys may have been for the nobility, a poor man's version would be home-made. A spinning top is mentioned in a story dating from about 1060; an example was found at Winchester which had been made from maple wood.

Toy knights, each clothed in armour and carrying a sword, have been found dating from the reign of Edward I. These must also have been mass-produced as they were metal and made from a mould. Girls had dolls – a tradition that is still with us; they were called poppets and were often made of wood. Some home-made poppets were very simple, other were manufactured and were much more handsome. There were also toy kitchen-sets manufactured which were moulded from a lead and tin alloy.

There were other games our children would recognise whose only value was in the pure fun of playing. Cherry stones were rolled or flipped into a 'cherry hole' in a game called 'cherry pit'. Nuts and stones were used in the same way: a pile of nuts was made and a nut would be thrown at the heap, the thrower then gathering up the scattered ones. Knuckle-bones were used for the game of 'fives' and the Luttrell Psalter has a picture showing children engaged in a piggy-back fight.

In the twelfth century, young lads played a game called knights with plantains, similar to the game of conkers. A dictionary was compiled for children in 1440; in it are mentioned children playing shuttle (cock) swinging on a swing and a see-saw which is called a merry-totter. It appears that children also competed at stone throwing and wrestling. So it was not all doom, gloom and a work laden existence for children in their early years.

A local legend

Those same children might well have been amused by a ceremony which began about 300 years after the Templars had disappeared from their Penhill Preceptory and which still continues today. It takes place in and around West Witton, only a short distance from the remains of the Penhill chapel, and is known as 'The Burning of Bartle'. Each year a straw effigy is carried through the village and the following verse is recited outside pubs and some houses:

> On Penhill Crags he tore his rags
> At Hunters Thorn he blew his horn
> At Capplebank Stee he brak' his knee
> At Grassgill Beck he brak' his neck
> At Wadhams End he couldn't fend
> At Grassgill End we'll mak' his end
> Shout, lads, Shout!

It is thought that Bartle may have been a notorious local sheep thief who was caught by the farmers whose livestock he stole after they had chased him down from Penhill. Another version of the tale has it that he was a giant who lived on Penhill, stole pigs and terrorised the neighbourhood. Either way, the effigy ends up on a bonfire every year on the Saturday nearest to 24 August, St Bartholomew's Day.

High up at the top of Penhill is a cairn of stones which marks the place where a beacon was lit. Or is this a pile of stones just waiting for the giant's children to come and play at knocking it down?

4

TEMPLE HIRST

(near Selby c. 1152)

Temple Hirst sits in the midst of farming country; the fields are flat and seemingly endless, but end they do in a vision of twenty-first century murkiness. Each way you look from Temple Hirst, the near horizon is thick with clouds emanating from two enormous power stations; a certain blot on the landscape in this area. The fields are still cultivated in much the same way as when the Templars were in residence, grain grown in a quiet tranquil hamlet. Though the mill is missing and almost all of the preceptory, it is easy to envisage an earlier industrious and productive time in this sleepy village.

The preceptory

The Templars settled here in about 1152 with the grant by Ralph and William Hastings being confirmed in 1155 by the superior lord of the Hastings family, Henry de Lacy. The de Lacy charter of confirmation still exists. It seems that the preceptory was fully operational by 1160 as records show that Robert Pirou was the preceptor. By the time of the 1185 Inquest, Temple Hirst had done very well in receiving gifts of land, including land at Norton 1160–70 and Eggborough 1161–77; Eggborough power station may possibly stand on what was once Templar lands! Then came land in Kellington and later the church at Kellington, 40 acres at Fenwick near Doncaster given by Foliot to provide for a chaplain and Burghwallis, to name just some of the gifts. Robert de Stapleton also donated land; he gave the vill of Osmundethorp to the Templars at Temple Hirst, which is a surprise since Osmundethorp is so close to Temple Newsam. Apparently in 1172, de Stapleton had exchanged 2 tofts in Pontefract for 3 bovates of land at Osmundethorp with the monks at Pontefract and this is where this land came from. He had already established a Chauntry at Thorpe Stapleton near Temple Newsam, swearing fealty to the Knights Templar and reserving all the offerings to the mother church at Whitechurche (Whitkirk).

A much later benefactor was John de Curteney who gave a parcel of land in East Hirst which butted up the dyke which ran from the Templar lands to Carlton. In the same charter, he also gave up all the rights which he had in the Templar woods.

There is a drain, which almost certainly had been constructed by the Templars, to the west of the property flowing to Temple Clough to drain lands. This is perfectly sound notion given that the area is so flat.

Temple Hirst's 'blot on the landscape' at Eggborough, seen from the River Aire near the former preceptory's site.

During excavations of St Edmund's Church at Kellington in 1990–91, a platform from the late Saxon period was discovered and it appears that the Knights Templar made substantial alterations to the church; further alterations were made when the church came into the hands of the Knights Hospitaller.

Only a little remains of the preceptory – just a Norman doorway which is built into the current dwelling of Preceptory Farm. The nursing home of Temple Manor next to the farm was also originally part of the preceptory. Although the tower which can be seen at Temple Manor has been described as part of the preceptory, it is not. The tower was originally built in the fifteenth or sixteenth century, then rebuilt probably in the seventeenth century, but may have reused medieval materials. Other features, such as a large barn, were pulled down in the twentieth century; this had been identified during the nineteenth century and had been mentioned in the 1185 Inquest, described as a large barn or grange. Other buildings mentioned were a chapel, stables, a bake- and brewhouse and a dormitory.

There is evidence to suggest that there had been a moat and outer defences surrounding the preceptory; with such a flat environment, such defences would have been deemed a necessity. Also, it appears that there are remains of a ford with Roman tiles embedded on an edge along the water course. These Roman tiles are still churned up now and then when ploughing takes place. It is thought that the tiles are the remains of a Roman road, possibly part of the Watling Street.

Temple Hirst preceptory lives on in the name of the farm which now occupies its former site.

In 1964, an in-depth survey was undertaken. From this work, together with aerial photographs taken in 1948, it is fairly certain that there were fishponds to the east of the preceptory which would fit in with the designs known at other preceptories and not, as some have suggested, a sixteenth-century formal garden.

On the opposite side of the road to where the gates at Temple Hirst Preceptory had been, there was a croft and windmill. These were apparently granted to the Templars by Milo de Stapleton. With so much arable land being worked, this would have been a boon for the Order.

In 1337, King Edward III granted the land of Temple Hirst to the Darcy family who retained it until Thomas Lord Darcy (mentioned in Chapter 5) was executed in 1537 for his part in for his part in the Pilgrimage of Grace in 1536.

Crime & punishment

The various crimes and methods of punishment were even more varied than they are today and most certainly, punishment was more grisly, with gruesome results.

Crime and punishment during the Templar timeline can roughly be divided into two eras: the time prior to the ascension of King Henry II in 1154 and afterwards. The significance of King Henry to crime was that he very quickly introduced changes to restore law and order to England. During the time of his predecessor, King Stephen, the barons had, among other things, proceeded to build castles without his express permission. King Henry ordered that the castles should be pulled down in order to bring the barons under control and bid them to respect his law. But the most significant and far reaching decision by the king was to put an end to the barbaric custom of trial by ordeal. He ordered that his own judges should be sent from London to listen to cases throughout the realm.

Trial by ordeal was not stamped out completely, as many manors held their own courts in the winter months. In 1215, Pope Innocent III decided that priests in England should not participate any longer in trials by ordeal. Following this, all trials were decided by judge and jury. Some time after 1275, a law was passed that allowed people to be tortured if they refused to go before a judge and jury.

The Church had its own courts which tried crimes of a religious nature, such as failure to attend church, blasphemy and of course, anything to do with the clergy that required discipline. The Church also offered sanctuary to criminals both real and imagined. Anyone could claim sanctuary by running to a church and making the claim. Pursuers could not enter the church to follow the felon. Offenders were then allowed to leave but had to also leave the country. Many churches and cathedrals had 'sanctuary' door knockers for use by those fleeing the law.

The physical correction of wives owed much to the old Roman law which allowed men to kill their wives for adultery. A double standard existed whereby the man of the household could take a maidservant for his pleasure without fear of retribution, though if a woman was found to have attempted an abortion, then she could be whipped and exiled.

Robber knights and barons were a phenomenon of the Middle Ages; this was eventually bought under control by the might of kings and by the increasing gentility of manners and the courtly code.

Some of the ordeals were quite hideous: peeping toms having their eye put out, while nose slitting for condoned adultery in marriage was common; the cutting off of other body parts, like a hand for theft; impaling with a red hot poker through the rectum, sometimes exiting through the victim's mouth; and a hamstring cut to produce a cripple whose life thereafter would be one of hunger and a very difficult existence.

Water and fire were commonly used to determine guilt or innocence of an accused. The person would have to either carry a red hot rod for three paces or walk across red hot ploughshares (the hardened blade of a plough). The distance depended on the seriousness of the crime. The hands or feet would be bound for three days; if the wound was healing, then innocence was declared, or guilt was proven if the wounds were not seen to be healing.

Punishment with water was equally horrid: the accused could be thrown into the water bound head and foot; if they floated, this would prove their guilt; if they sank, their innocence. Boiling water was also used: the accused would have to fast for three days, then they took part in mass. For a minor offence, the accused immersed their hand to the wrist in boiling water, often to retrieve a stone; the more serious the offence, the further up the arm would be immersed.

For rape, murder, abduction or treason, a number of punishments were performed. One was to have each limb tied to separate horses and each horse was then made to run in a different direction. Women who were accused of murder would be strangled and then burned.

There were so many people who lost limbs or were mutilated in some way through legitimate causes at work that they could apply for a paper stating this fact in order not to be mistaken for miscreants.

If accused of something, nobles could opt for combat with the person who made the allegation. This quite simply meant a fight to the death, with the winner being judged to be in the right. This was a custom which came over with the Normans.

Most men carried knives in the Middle Ages, but these were merely a tool for work, and for eating food and not for fighting with.

Often those who were deemed guilty of a crime would be summarily committed to hanging as there were few prisons and, in any case, communities were loath to pay for a prisoner's upkeep; it was cheaper to execute the guilty party.

Most towns had a gibbet; mostly, people were hanged on these and their bodies left to rot over the following weeks as a warning to others.

Halifax was an exception the rule of a gibbet used for hanging. There, a blade was inserted and a contraption devised so that no person actually 'put their hand to kill another' at the gibbet. It is thought that Halifax was granted the 'privilege' of a gibbet as early as 1066, shortly after the Norman invasion, though this is unsubstantiated, and the earliest recorded reference is 1280. At the time, about 100 other gibbets were recorded and this rather dubious privilege was 'enjoyed' in Yorkshire. Halifax was then a small hamlet with only about fifteen cottages; its setting and status came about because of its wealth of clear water. It was an ideal location for the early cloth trade. Fearful of increased crime in the developing trade, the gibbet privilege passed from the Crown to the bailiff of the manor. Eventually, all beheadings took place at the Saturday market to take advantage of the increased attendance.

The only way a condemned man could beat the gibbet at Halifax was to pull back his head as the blade fell. Then he needed to effect an escape by running over the parish boundary by way of the Hebble stream, roughly a mile away. Two men did escape in this way; one by the name of Dinnis and one called John Lacey. Lacey made the mistake of returning to Halifax seven years later and was duly executed without trial. A public house, the Running Man, commemorates the fact.

The blade from the gibbet is housed in the Bankfield Museum in Halifax. It weighs just over 7lbs and is about 10in in length. There is still a mock gibbet in Halifax which can be seen in Gibbet Street.

The last gibbet in use was in Leicester in 1832. On 10 August, one James Cook was convicted of a particularly grisly murder. His head was shaved and after he was hanged, the head was tarred to prevent weathering. It was then displayed on purpose-built gallows, with a view to leave it there to rot. Thousands of people

Halifax gibbet.

came to view the ghastly sight, much to the annoyance of the local residents. It was finally removed on the following Tuesday after much complaint from the locals. Gibbeting was no longer legal after a change in the law in 1843.

Some members of society were ostracised because of their trade or lifestyle. These included the tanners and skinners and the knackers (horse slaughterers). These people normally lived on the edges of towns and villages. However, we know that on many Templar sites, the tanners lived within the confines of the preceptory. Then there were the tinkers and gypsies who took to the road. Vagabonds and beggars also stayed on the outside of towns. All these people were vulnerable to be preyed upon by bandits. Bandits were mostly drawn from deserters or discharged soldiers who had retained their arms, the modern equivalent of gangsters.

It would be reasonable to think that with such hideous punishments, which had the sole aim of keeping law and order, relatively few crimes were committed. However, in Lincoln in 1202 the city had 114 murders, eighty-nine violent robberies and sixty-five people were wounded in fights. Amazingly, only two people were executed for their crimes.

The death penalty for murder was repealed in 1965.

Death: beliefs & rituals

Upon death, it was thought that the soul exited the body through the mouth; cinema imagery often depicts this still. The general population were wrapped in simple shrouds for interment. When a person thought he was near to death, he would take to his bed and bid his family to say their farewell, with the local priest giving absolution.

A sudden death was much feared; in order to help prevent this from occurring, it was believed that St Christopher could help. A painting of the saint was often to be found on a wall opposite the church door. When people passed by, they could look at the painting and believe they were protected against sudden death for that day.

It was considered wise and correct form to have your estates in good order and to have written a will prior to death. When illness struck which would result in death, a will had to be written about ten days before the time of the expected demise.

Noble families wrote their wills years in advance, much the same as today. Nobility often left instructions as to where they wanted their body interred. This frequently meant quite a lot of effort on the part of the family. For instance, Gilbert de Clare died in Brittany but he wished to be buried in Tewksbury Abbey. Therefore, his entire household had to make the arduous journey to carry out his wishes.

These instructions were not always carried out though; the most famous case of the wishes of the departed being ignored involved King Edward I and King Edward II.

Edward I requested that his heart should be sent to Palestine and his body boiled in a large cauldron, his flesh then be buried and his bones carried into battle against the Scots. In fact, his son, King Edward II, did none of these things. He had his father's complete body interred in a rather ordinary tomb in Westminster Abbey.

When a monk felt close to death, he sent for the abbot; then the monk was taken from his bed to confess his sins to the entire community of monks. After this very public confession, he was returned to his bed. The monk then received communion and psalms would be read. There was also a procession of servers carrying candles, holy water and a cross. Lighted candles were put at either end of his bed and monks from the infirmary would stay with him until he passed away, when he would be laid on a sackcloth and ashes in the shape of a cross. Prayers were then said to accompany his departing soul.

The general belief in the eleventh, twelfth and thirteenth centuries was that at the Last Judgement, souls would be divided between those who journeyed on to heaven and those who descended into hell. Later, intercessors were involved, including Christ, Mary and myriad saints. Later, a courtroom image became the representation, with God sitting on high passing out the sentences to the souls.

Purgatory was thought to be the waiting area for souls situated between earth and heaven. Continual prayers said by the living for the dead departed were thought to have the effect of lessening the waiting time and to help cleanse the soul of any misdemeanours.

Chapels outnumbered churches in the Middle Ages in many country areas. For instance, in Lancashire, there were 100 detached chapels in fifty-nine parishes, while in Cornwall, there were over 700 chapels in 204 parishes. These chapels were often a long way from the parishes' churches. Since death and burial was a profitable income, there was often friction between chapel and church for the right to burials. Quite often the chapel was under the jurisdiction of a powerful overlord, or as we have seen in other chapters, the Templars were given rights not always bestowed on other ecclesiastical orders.

People were originally buried inside the church but as these places filled up, burials took place in the churchyard and from there to cemeteries where the land was blessed by the bishop. However, if the area was polluted, for example, by the spilling of blood, it meant that the churchyard became inoperable for about two years during which time burials were unable to take place until it had been spiritually cleared by the bishop.

At Beverly in East Yorkshire, the Minster churchyard was sprinkled with water blessed by the Archbishop of York; it was an expensive affair. Forty shillings had to be paid to the archbishop, 5 shillings to the marshal and 2 shillings to the clerk.

In 1206, Pope Innocent III granted rights to the local churches for the burial of sailors who had drowned on the east coast.

Death during the crusades was a difficult matter. Many remained where they fell, although if someone of importance fell, it may have been different. There are cases where bodies were conveyed all the way back to England from the Holy Land. John de Ros died in Cyprus and was carried back to England to be buried at Rievaux Abbey in North Yorkshire. One alternative was to be buried in the country where you died and later to be disinterred, as with John de Mowbray; killed by the Turks and buried first by the Dominican monks in Galatia, he was later disinterred and brought to England. Another method was to have the heart cut out and sent to England in a casket.

This carrying of a heart in a casket was not confined to fallen crusaders; Lady Devorgilla carried the heart of her husband, John Balliol, in a casket. She founded Sweetheart Abbey in 1273 in memory of her much loved husband and upon her death, she was laid to rest with the casket in the abbey. Her husband's name is remembered much more for his involvement with Oxford University. Edward I stayed at Sweetheart Abbey in 1300.

The Church & science

To say that the medieval population was superstitious is an understatement. This was fuelled by the Church who were not at all sympathetic to any 'modern' teaching, always fearing that new ideas would run contrary to the teachings of the Church, which they often did.

With the translation of Aristotle's *Physics and Metaphysics* in the thirteenth century, the battle between Church and science had begun in earnest. A progression of secular knowledge carried with it a disparaging view towards the Church and its conservatism of learned modernism by scholars, both outside and inside the secular circle. The Church frowned upon pursuits of almost all scientific leanings. Many Arabic translations were at the bottom of this displeasure. This included Aristotle's theory of the 'Four Elements' which in turn, produced theories of transmuting matter, the search for the component parts of the 'Philosopher's Stone' and of matters relating to alchemy. This suspicion of the alchemist was fuelled by the secrecy and shielding of the symbolic representations used by them. Substances were clothed in certain colours and icons represented different metals. Many alchemists were idealists but equally, many were cheats and phoneys swindling their clients by pretending to be able to turn base metal in to gold. It seems the desire to 'make a quick buck' was, and is, firmly entrenched in the human psyche.

A deep-seated belief of this time was taken from Plato – 'as above, so below' – or, in the larger picture of the universe is to be found the smaller picture of each individual and that man and the universe corresponded with nature and structure.

5

TEMPLE NEWSAM

(near Leeds, c. 1154)

Today, the name Temple Newsam House evokes a scene fit for a television drama. This was a huge mansion house built in the late fifteenth century by Thomas Lord Darcy (who was later beheaded) and situated within 1,500 acres of parkland. It is of Tudor-Jacobean design with a host of history attached; the birthplace of Lord Darnley, infamous husband of Mary Queen of Scots and Lord Charles Stuart are perhaps the most notable of its occupants. The house had at first private and then public ownership and now draws large numbers of visitors, encourages school children to learn a little of their heritage, hosts concerts and generally is on the radar of the Leeds heritage trail.

The preceptory

However, prior to all the pomp and splendour of the current dwelling, there was an earlier ownership. Not far from the present house in what is now farmland, there was a Knights Templar preceptory which came into being around 1154. In order to understand about the preceptory, we need to go back a little further in time. Before William I, better known as William the Conqueror, the area was owned by Dunstan and Glunier, Anglo-Saxon thanes, meaning they were of Saxon nobility. Indeed, one find on this site was a latrine, radio carbon dated to the ninth or tenth century, confirming that the area was inhabited during the Anglo-Saxon era. It was then known by the name of Neuhusum as shown in the Domesday Book.

By 1086 the area belonged to, but was not owned by, Ilbert de Lacey who had followed William into battle against the English twenty years earlier. We will come across Ilbert and the Lacey family a number of times in the following pages. Ilbert was made an English baron about 1072 for services rendered.

Around 1155 the Neuhusum area passed to the Knights Templar, though in some quarters a charter states that the Templars were granted free warren as late as 1248. Temple Newsam was acquired by the Templars in a complex way, a combination of gift, purchase and grant. Part of the land was gifted to them by William de Villiers, who had rented the land from Henry de Lacey (or Lascy), part was exchanged for land previously gifted to them at Newbold in Nottinghamshire and part was purchased. According to the 1185 Inquest, the land had been purchased by the Knights Templar. Purchasing was a common way for the Templars to obtain land;

however, it is not possible to show the acreage for each parcel of land acquired by the Order at Temple Newsam. It is known that they would purchase land adjacent to gifted land that was often of poor quality or quite uncultivated, but that did have potential and would lead to a navigable river – in this case the Aire. The following is the charter of Henry de Lascy:

Henry de Lascy to his venerable father, Roger, Archbishop of York, and to all other sons of holy mother church present as well as future, greeting. Be it known to you all that I gave and by this my charter have confirmed to God and to Holy Mary and to the brethren of the Temple of Solomon the land which William de Vilers gave to them in perpetual alms, to wit Niehus and Scheltunam and Choletunam and Wite chirche [Newsam, Skelton, Colton and Whitkirk] with all their appurtenances in wood, in plain, in meadow, in waters, in mills, in fisheries, in footpaths, within and without the way. And know ye that I gave them this land in exchange for the land of Nieuboud which I first gave to them, and these brethren have returned to me that land of Nieuboud which, in the same way, I gave to Widon de la Vale. But I gave this land to the aforesaid brethren in perpetual alms, free and exempt from all secular tribute and service, as free and undisturbed as they hold any land, freer and more undisturbed than was the case in the time of Henry the King. And know ye that I and my heirs guarantee this land to the said brethren against all men. But I have done this for the good of my soul and for the souls of my father and mother and of all my friends as well living as dead, that it may give everlasting life to us. But this covenant was made in the presence of the lord king. These are witnesses: William de Vescy, Jordan Foliot, Robert Pictavensis, Ralph de Tielli, William de Rienvilla, Oto de Tielli, Henry Foliot, Richard Bacod, Henry Walensis, Robert Barbo, Henry de Dai, William de Rie, William de Budli, Thomas filius Petri.

Henry de Lascy had to confirm the *grant* of land as he was de Villiers' superior lord. The land, previously assigned to his grandfather Ilbert, had passed to Henry, who was of an established noble Norman family. All of his lands had been directly granted to him by King Henry I, second son of William the Conqueror.

As a matter of interest, Henry de Lacey also founded a Cistercian Order at Kirkstall Abbey around 1152 after recovering from an illness. There are many road names in the Kirkstall area harking back to the de Lacey name.

The nobility & land grants

The following is a brief explanation about grants, which was fundamental to the feudal system introduced by William the Conqueror, a system that persisted for a number of centuries.

William granted huge tracts of English lands to the faithful French nobles made up of dukes, earls and barons who had followed him into battle and had thereby demonstrated their loyalty to him. Although the size of these lands was equal to the size of counties today, the lands did not consist of actual counties. In return for the land 'granted' to them, they had to swear an oath of allegiance and also, in a sense, govern those areas in William's stead. Some of the things these nobles were expected to do were to collect taxes, provide soldiers if required by the king, and generally ensure the heel of the Normans was felt by the English people, crushing any rebellion before it took hold.

Although the nobles did not pay rent as we know it for their lands, the taxes collected went to the king, who was deemed to be the real owner of the land. After the due taxes were paid, the lord of the land was able to keep anything left over in terms of money and stock.

To make a brutal point, William set about bringing part of his new realm to heel by crushing the particularly mutinous northerners. He carried out a scorched earth policy which rendered much of the land useless. It was to be many years before the results of this course of action were remedied.

The areas granted to the nobles were still rather large and difficult to manage, so once the land had been parcelled out to the nobles, they in turn allocated land to those who had served them well. These were lesser nobles and knights, who then swore fealty to their superior lord. All these oaths were sworn on the Bible, a big issue in medieval times, as few would break such an oath, lest they were condemned to hell. Religion was a huge part of everyone's life. It is difficult now to imagine how influential religion was in their lives from the king down to the lowliest peasant. The population was much smaller then, but religion had a much bigger impact on their lives. A peasant could have his ear cut off for not attending church!

So each knight had a sector of land to administer and do exactly as his sovereign lord did; collect taxes and provide men for service to the king when necessary. It was seen that having sworn fealty to his superior lord he had, in effect, sworn the oath to the king himself. They were also expected to give provision and lodging for a knight and provide training or money to equip a knight in time of war. With the land went all the people on it. The superior lord was known as a tenant-in-chief and the knights as sub-tenants. This was why Ilbert did not *own* the land and why Henry I was able to *grant* the land to Henry de Lacey, Ilbert's grandson.

Templar tenants

When the Templars acquired their land near Leeds, they called it Newsam meaning 'New House'. The preceptory was constructed between 1154 and 1165. When the land was gifted, a document called a charter was drawn up; this one was executed at Pontefract Castle by Henry de Vernoils and is shown earlier in this chapter. A papal bull required the Knights Templar to be free of tithes and taxes, and this was embodied in the charter. For example, mill owners were able to charge and tax others for the use of the mill, but could not charge the Templars. By contrast, the Templars *were* able to charge such taxes for the use of their mills. So they were gifted the land without encumbrance. 'For the salvation of my soul' was also inserted in the charter; this meant that prayers were said for the benefactor and his family on a regular basis. It was a legally binding requirement and would probably be written into a charter for lands gifted to almost any religious order.

The area around Temple Newsam had suffered from the scorched earth policy twenty years earlier, so the Templars needed to restore the land for agricultural use and to build their preceptory and associated buildings. During the excavations of 1991, archaeologists found the foundations of a huge barn about 150ft long. It had aisles down the sides, with the roof supported by wooden posts standing on pieces of stone compacted together in a shallow well of earth. From the measurements, the barn must have been a very large building. A number of pits were also found.

Temple Newsam is close to the River Aire, a sizeable water source. Traces of ditches were found during the excavations of 1991, so a water course may have been dug from the River Aire to the encampment. There was a variety of land types within the whole area which consisted of woodland, arable land, meadows, pastures, the river and fisheries. These were considered important at the time. In the charter, all the various types of land were listed for legal reasons; this made it quite clear that the Templars were being granted everything without exception.

Near Newsam township they held 16 carucates of land (nearly 2,000 acres), of which 6 carucates and 3 bovates were retained for their own use. They also received an income in cash, kind and labour from the following tenants in the vicinity:

> Baldwin rented 1 bovate for 2½ shillings and 2 hens, 20 eggs and 4 boonworks. His work allocation for the Templars included ploughing, harrowing, scything, making hay, work to make pond repairs, to carry millstones, and to wash sheep one day and shear them the other.
> Bertram and Osbert rented 1 bovate for 30 pennies and aforesaid services.
> Robert of Hammerton and the aforesaid Osbert rented 1 bovate for 30 pennies and aforesaid services.
> Warner rented 2 bovates for 5 shillings and aforesaid services.
> Richard Kemp rented 1 bovate for 30 pennies and aforesaid services.
> Richard and Robert White rented 1 bovate and 1 acre for 3s and aforesaid services.
> William Coli rented 1 bovate for 30 pennies and aforesaid services.
> Richard Franceis rented 1 bovate for 30 pennies and aforesaid services.
> Reginald Vavasour rented 1 bovate for 30 pennies and aforesaid services.
> Robert Brun rented 1 bovate for 30 pennies and aforesaid services.
> Joseph rented 1 bovate for 30 shillings and aforesaid services and 2½ acres for 15 pennies and 2 hens, 20 eggs and 6 boonworks.

Joseph rented 2½ acres for 15d and 2 hens and 10 eggs and 6 boonworks.

Hugh, 2 acres for 12 pennies and 1 hen and 10 eggs and 4 boonworks.

Qurand, 2 acres for 12 pennies and aforesaid services.

Randulph Panche, 2 acres for 12 pennies and aforesaid services.

It was stipulated that all cottars also had to take part in hay spreading and making once, plus sheep washing and shearing and pond repairs, just the same as those who held 1 bovate of land.

Land measurements such as carucates and bovates were rough calculations of how much land a team of eight oxen could plough in a year. A carucate is approximately 120 acres and a bovate about an eighth of that, roughly 15 acres.

The term 'boonworks', mentioned above as part of Baldwin's rent, means the provision of free labour from time to time. The lord (or in this case the Knights Templar) would decide when those days would be used. As can be seen from the work Baldwin had to carry out, these boon days were principally used to advantage during the busy seasons of the agricultural year. It wasn't all bad, though. It was often the custom for the workers to be provided with free food and drink for the day, so at least there was some compensation. On the whole, villagers were tied to the land and to the lord; they had little say in the day-to-day workings of their lives.

Templar farming

The Templars were exemplary in their farming methods. They followed a practice of working the large farms themselves and subletting the small crofts and farms, which were often scattered and isolated. This made the smaller properties viable and profitable for the Templars.

The larger farms which they worked were always profitable. The Templars regenerated the land from the scorched earth policy and nursed the soil back to usefulness. They grew crops on the arable land and it is thought to have been a four crop rotation of possibly wheat, oats, peas or beans and fallow. Meadows were used for lower-grade crop production, including hay as a winter crop for animal feed.

A high production of oats were grown (as they were at all Yorkshire sites) which indicate that the Templars fed their stock throughout the winter instead of slaughtering them, which was the more usual practice. England as a whole was a prime source, through the Templars, of agricultural wealth as well as capitalising on the revenue generated by the wool trade.

The development of the Order's wool trade mirrored that of the Cistercians, also founded primarily by St Bernard of Clairvaux. The pastures, essentially in the more rough and spartan areas, were home to over 1,000 head of sheep. Fleeces were an early key to the wealth of the Templar Order, sending the special long stranded wool to Flanders, Lille or Arras. This would imply that the return obtained from the sale of wool was more valuable than the cultivation of a cash crop such as wheat. The size of the barn, as mentioned earlier, would have taken large quantities of winter food storage to maintain the sheep throughout the winter.

The Templar Order had a variety of other ways to earn income for their Brethren; advowsons from rectories and churches, rents from houses and tenements, banking, services and tributes from the tenants, taxes from wind, water and fulling mills, and from fairs and markets, to name a few. The profit made was not for the personal use of the Templars, but was sent to London to the Temple headquarters and distributed for the needs of the Brothers in the East.

Woodland was a very important part of the land-holding. Timber was used for building purposes and trees were coppiced for poles and handles. Charcoal was also produced from the woodland. Pigs were reared and grazed in the woods, though strictly controlled to prevent over-grazing.

The river was also vital to the Templar community in many ways. Apart from the clear need for water on the domestic front, it was an essential food source. The River Aire was divided along the stretch between Leeds and Rothwell for several fisheries. Fishponds were constructed to breed fish for the table if the river was a considerable distance away from the living quarters.

Fulling procedures

One of the most important river uses was for mills. Temple Newsam had three, two for corn and one for fulling. Together with several other places in England, Temple Newsam claims to have had the first fulling mill. There was certainly a mill there when the Templars carried out the survey of all their possessions in 1185, but it was probably established much earlier than that.

It's very likely that this type of mill was invented in England and its appearance would not have gone down well in some quarters. Prior to its invention, the fulling process was carried out by unskilled workers, while the use of fulling mills meant that large numbers of these workers found themselves without a job and at a time when food prices were escalating. At the beginning of the thirteenth century, the average wage for an unskilled worker was around 12 pennies per week which would have bought him one sheep and not much else. To put this in perspective, the cost of a sheep in 2006 was about £100, while an unskilled labourer earning the minimum wage today would bring home little more than £200 per week.

Before the arrival of the medieval fulling mill, fullers had the unpleasant task of tramping up and down for two hours per length of cloth, in water containing either fuller's earth or stale urine. This had the effect of softening the cloth by drawing out the lanolin from the wool. The water-driven fulling mills were much more efficient, using heavy wooden hammers to achieve the same effect. Fulling fabric still takes place today as a method of cleaning, shrinking and thickening cloth.

The pits found in the 1991 excavation show a white limy substance that may have been used for a tanning process for the removal of hair and flesh remains from animal skins, indicating again a need for quantities of water. There were also pits thought to have been used for the storage of shellfish (one presumes freshwater variety), freshwater fish and of course, drinking water.

Slag was found on the site and there was, and still is, outcropping of coal. Where outcropping was close to a water source, then the coal could be recovered for use quite easily. It is thought that the coal would only have been used for personal consumption to augment the wood fires and not for commercial use. That was saved for British Coal!

Village hierarcy

As was seen earlier, people were part of the deal when land was either purchased or gifted, so the Templars had a ready supply of workers. A function of the villagers was to work on the farms, tanneries, fisheries etc. to cultivate for the Templars as with any other manorial lord. The villagers also had a piece of land to work for themselves. Part would be on arable soil and part on poor soil to ensure that the workers had equal land output to help with their subsistence.

At the height of its productivity, there would have been many different trades going on at Temple Newsam. For example, there may have been a farrier, baker, farmers, shepherd, blacksmith and possibly an armourer. The average payment for some trades around 1308 would have been: servants 3 pennies per day, gardener 2 pennies per day and a mason the princely sum of 4 pennies per day.

There was a hierarchy of villagers. Cottars were of the lowest social standing and would be entitled to use only a small amount of land to grow crops to eat or to sell. Sometimes they would have no land at all; in that case, all they could do was hire themselves out and try to make a living that way. At the other end of the scale were sokemen. These were freemen who paid in cash or kind for the land they rented. In between these two extremes were villeins who were bound to the land and were not permitted to leave and farm somewhere else. Their landholding in the village's fields would be substantial; they would, however, also have to work on the land belonging to the lord of the manor.

Inhabitants of the preceptory, as stipulated by the Rule, were divided between knights, sergeants, chaplains and free servants. Included in the Temple Newsam community would have been the preceptor and a couple of Brethren administrators, a chaplain, pilgrims and Brethren on their travels. Lay persons often served for years as free servants and were frequently rewarded for their service by being given pensions, clothing and food at the free persons' table in the refectory.

Templar rules

The Templars at Newsam, as with everyone in the Order, were compelled to follow the rules laid down by St Bernard of Clairvaux. For instance, they were honour-bound to take one-tenth of their food and give it to the poor and needy and/or any wayfarers who may have to lodge with them overnight. At dusk, at the behest of King Stephen, it was the practice to blow a horn so that nearby pilgrims or travellers would know they were welcome for food and a bed for the night.

Another rule prohibited hunting, stating:

We collectively forbid any brother to hunt a bird with another bird. It is not fitting for a man of religion to succumb to pleasures, but to hear willingly the commandments of God, to be often in prayer and each day to confess tearfully to God in his prayers the sins he has committed . . . we command especially all brothers not to go in to the woods with a longbow or crossbow to hunt animals or to accompany anyone who would do so . . . nor shout or chatter, nor to spur a horse out of desire . . .

This prohibition did not extend to their tenants. Templars were, however, told that the ban on hunting did not include the lion 'for he come encircling and searching for what he can devour . . .'

Whitkirk

The Templars at Newsam also owned Whitkirk, as well as other land and goods mentioned later in this chapter. At that time Whitkirk was purely a parish and not a village, and there was no hint of it becoming the suburb of Leeds that it is today. The church was close to Colton on the border of Halton and Austhorpe, about a mile from the preceptory.

The Brethren employed their own chaplain there, Paulinus, whom they paid 3 marks a year. (To put this in context, his annual salary would have bought him about fifteen live sheep.) His stipend would have come out of the 'altarage', which was the profit made from gifts, donations and tithes paid by the congregation. He was fortunate. At that time, not every clergyman received remuneration for the services he rendered. However, this changed after 1215 when they were all required to be paid from the Church's income. Another Whitkirk priest that we know of during Templar times was Elias. He served at the church during the late twelfth or early thirteenth century and is mentioned in a deed which he witnessed.

The Templars would not recognise the present church of St Mary at Whitkirk. Some rebuilding took place in the mid-eighteenth and early nineteenth centuries, with major alterations occurring in 1980. It is thought that the site had been a place of worship long before the Normans arrived, and there had probably been a wooden structure there. After that, it's likely that a white stone building was erected; hence the name 'Witechirche' which later became Whitekirk, before settling down to become Whitkirk. The Domesday Book shows the church as originally belonging to the manor and berewick of Gipton and Colton, a berewick being the outlying property of a manor.

St Mary's wasn't the only Templar-related place of worship in the parish. Towards the end of the twelfth century, Sir Robert de Stapleton had approached the Master of the Temple in London requesting permission to build a chapel in Thorpe Stapleton. This was agreed on condition that all offerings received there would go to St Mary's. In addition, he had to swear fealty to the Order of the Knights Templar. The area in which the chapel stood was between the south western edge of the Temple Newsam estate and a loop in the River Aire at Rothwell. The settlement itself still existed in 1822 with a complement of three houses and a map

St Mary's Church, Whitkirk.

of the area in 1852 shows Thorpe Hall still standing. All that remains today is the south wall of the Elizabethan manor house.

Robert de Stapleton was also involved in another transaction with the Templars. He granted them the vill of nearby Osmondthorpe. In 1269 they also acquired 4 tofts (a toft is a homestead, its outbuildings and enclosed land), 4 bovates, 8 acres of land and 4 acres of meadow from Adam de Ryther and his wife, Juliana.

Colton

The Templars also had tenants at Colton, which was more extensive in those days than it is now. However, the medieval settlement, built in the twelfth century, was situated centrally on the northern border of the Temple Newsam estate – a different location from the modern village. The reason for this is that after the repression of the Order, Temple Newsam passed into private hands and between 1489 and 1490, the estate was emparked. Strictly speaking, if an estate was enclosed to contain deer, a royal licence had to be obtained. This was because all deer were considered to be the property of the Crown. Sometimes areas were emparked simply to due to an increasing fashion for the aristocracy to show their ownership of grand country mansions. Either way, emparkment led to whole villages being moved or destroyed to satisfy this vogue, a fate that befell the original village of Colton.

Archeological digs on the site in 1980 and 1993 identified post holes of the medieval wooden houses that made up the earlier settlement. The West Yorkshire Archeological Survey reports two superimposed buildings for the same period: 'The aisle posts were earth-fast and the primary phase single aisle-wall was of stud construction in shallow post-settings'. It goes on to report that a later building had a central hearth burnt into the natural clay, 'suggesting a double aisled building whose aisle-posts had rested on stylobates', a stylobate being the immediate foundation of a row of columns.

The Order also acquired holdings in Colton from people who were possibly descendants of tenants of William de Vilers, from whom they had acquired Newsam. A holding may even have previously belonged to a tenant of the Templars. Among the assets they received was one from Elizabeth, widow of Jordan de L'Isle, who transferred her right in lands in Colton to the Templars in 1257, so it's possible her late husband had been a tenant.

The 1185 Inquest shows that Cecilia of Campeus also donated land near Colton to the Knights Templar. This gift included various rents from her existing tenants. These were:

Richard, son of Arnald, who paid rent of 3 shillings for 1 bovate (about fifteen acres) and 2 acres 'and the same services which the men of Newsham make'.

Arnald, possibly Richard's father, rented 1 bovate, for 2 shillings and 'aforesaid services' (that is, the same as those mentioned for Temple Newsam).

Fulc paid 30 pence for 2 bovates, and 'aforesaid services'.

Then there was Waldin who, for 2 bovates and half his messuage because it was deserted, paid rent of 3 shillings for all services. [A messuage is a dwelling house including outbuildings, orchard, court-yard and garden.]

Finally, Thomas of L'Isle's 3 carucates (about 360 acres) were rented to him in return for 'foreign service'. Perhaps he was sent off to serve in some capacity for the Templars in the Middle East, but the Inquest does not specify exactly what 'foreign service' might have entailed.

It says something about the status of women that Cecilia's donation was confirmed by Thomas, her son. She must have been a widow at the time, because women were not allowed to own property of any kind unless they were widows. Nor could they inherit land from their parents if they had any surviving brothers.

Women, even of the highest rank, had few rights and privileges and their freedom was limited in medieval England. They would have worked alongside men on the land, but got paid less for their endeavours. Peasant women were generally older than their richer sisters when they married, as they were needed to continue working for the family as long as possible and thus augment its overall income. There was another financial implication too. A peasant would have had to pay a *merchet* to his lord upon the marriage of a daughter. This was because the lord was losing a worker so the father was, in effect, buying the right to give his daughter away to someone else.

Skelton

Southwest of Temple Newsam lies Skelton. It also fell victim to the emparkment which claimed the original village of Colton, although probably a bit later. The Templars owned an estimated 4 carucates of land which included the following rents, services and goods:

William of Granville, 3 bovates for no service.

Humfrai for 2 bovates a rent of 4 shillings, 4 hens, 40 eggs and 8 boonworks with 1 man in autumn, once to scythe and make hay, twice to plough and twice to harrow, once to wash and shear sheep, and to work at the mill.

Richard, son of Gamell, for 2 bovates a rent of 4 shillings and aforesaid services.

John, son of Gocelyn, for 2 bovates a rent of 4 shillings and aforesaid services.

Peter, son of Quenild, for 2 bovates, a rent of 4 shillings and aforesaid services.

Accra Jordan owes to the brothers on account of his poverty, 12 pennies and 4 boonworks and 1 hen and 10 eggs (which he was accustomed to pay).

John Fullo for 2 bovates, a rent of 4 shillings and aforesaid services.

Richard Nobil for ½ bovate, a rent of 2 shillings, 4 boonworks and aforesaid services.

Ailsi for 2 bovates, a rent of 4 shillings and aforesaid services.

Robert, son of Ailive, for 2 bovates a rent of 4 shillings and aforesaid services.

William, skinner, for 1 acre a rent of 10 pennies and 4 boonworks.

Gosse and Trig for 2 bovates, a rent of 4 shillings and aforesaid services.

Suanus for 2 bovates a rent of 4 shillings and aforesaid services.

Richard Nobil for 2 bovates, a rent of 4 shillings and aforesaid services.

Ivete for 2 bovates a rent of 4 shillings for all services.

Jordan for 2 bovates, a rent of 3 shillings for all services.

Gilbert, son of Walding, for 2 bovates, a rent of 4 shillings and aforesaid services.

Ailsi, son of John, for 2 bovates, a rent of 4 shillings and aforesaid services.

Osbert, son of Ralph, for 1 bovate for a rent of 2 shillings and aforesaid services.

Wlvive, widow, 1 dwelling house for nothing.

Dolfin for ½ carucate and 11 acres of church land, a rent of 9 shillings and 9½ pennies.

Halton

As we saw with Robert de Stapleton and his chapel, any transactions regarding holdings had to be carried out with the Knights Templar as an organisation, not with individual local preceptors. And so at some time between 1223 and 1228, an agreement was reached between Stephen, Abbot of Sallay (Sawley) Abbey and Alan Martel, Master of the Temple in London, regarding land at Halton. This is another Leeds suburb not far from Temple Newsam. The abbot let a farm to them consisting of all of its land and the men who lived there. The holding consisted of 5 carucates of land, a further 5 bovates of land and five parts of Halton Wood. A wood still exists at Halton Moor.

The annual rent was 10 marks, payment to be made at Newsam and the agreement was to be in force forever. After the suppression of the Knights Templar, Edward II gave temporary custody of the manor of Newsam to John de Argail, who was ordered to continue paying the rent due to Sawley Abbey.

Templars in central Leeds

The Temple Newsam Preceptory also owned holdings in the centre of the growing town of Leeds itself. Then, as now, Briggate was a busy thoroughfare and the Templars were participants in its growth and vitality more than 800 years ago.

Near the Headrow end of the road, they owned half a dozen buildings which housed their tenants. A Templar cross can still be seen attached to the end of a popular pub in the vicinity called The Pack Horse. There is also evidence that they may have had other tenants in central Leeds. There used to be more Templar crosses on buildings in Vicar Lane, Lower Headrow, Bridge Street, Lady Lane and the significantly named Templar Street. Unfortunately, all of these areas have been redeveloped and no crosses remain to be seen.

Templar cross on the wall of The Pack Horse public house, Briggate.

Example of a Templar cross on a dwelling house in the Bingley area.

Templar tenants all had these crosses attached to their buildings for one very good reason – money. The Templars, through their various charters, and with the blessing of both the Pope and their sovereign, were exempt from taxes that applied to the majority of other orders. This exemption, in many cases, also extended to the tenants of the Templars. It's small wonder, therefore, that some people attached crosses to their property when they had no right to do so. It was simply a medieval form of tax evasion!

6

FOULBRIDGE

(near Malton, c. 1177)

Foulbridge is a Templar site which sent tremors of excitement through the world of Knights Templar scholars. This medieval hall, part of which had been used as an apple store, had been shut off from the world for decades and was only rediscovered in 1981.

For 450 years, the large farm had been worked as two farms with two owners. The Nutt family had farmed there since 1948, first as tenants and later as owners. In due course, the family acquired both parts of the farm to reunite them under one ownership and as one farm. It was much later before they had the run of both parts of the homestead as the foreman occupied the other half of the building; he retired and the discovery was made. When Jill Nutt decided to give it a clean, a surprise was in store. It was through her curiosity of a white limy substance on a wooden post at the end of a small room that she thought needed closer inspection. Looking at it, Jill thought that something didn't quite look right as it was not reaching a natural finish. With the panache worthy of a television renovation team, she began to punch a hole through the surrounding plaster. Lo and behold there was a yawning space behind, thereby opening up the main section of the Foulbridge preceptory hall.

The preceptory

Like many places in the Vale of Pickering, once leaving the main road, within moments one feels isolated from the modern world. So it is with Foulbridge. Leaving the busy A64 trunk road which takes thousands of visitors to the holiday destinations of the east coast, one follows a small lane, overgrown with grasses in the centre and then cross a railway line. Instantly, seclusion permeates from the modern world, envelopes one and gives a glimpse of a remote and gentler lifestyle. Bypassing a couple of farms, through a farmyard, over wooden plank bridges, passing fields of wheat and a deep cut stream, one finally arrives at a splendid farm entrance that now counts a Templar Hall as part of its home comfort zone.

A huge pond in front of the farm attracts wildlife from the nearby stream. It is home to swans, trout and a whole host of birdlife, with a resident barn owl keeping a watchful eye over the proceedings. The pond reaches almost to an ancient wall, which may or may not have been the edge of a moat. It has been

White limy substance on a beam at Foulbridge.

suggested that Foulbridge was a moated preceptory, but it is not known for sure one way or the other.

If the Templars returned to Foulbridge, 700 hundred years on, they would find little has changed in the landscape. Just like Faxfleet, Foulbridge stands on ground that is slightly higher than the surrounding countryside. There are still numerous cultivated fields and although the course of the river may have changed a little, it still it meanders through them on its way to the sea. There are more trees to be seen around the preceptory and fewer buildings. And though these are very different from the original layout, it's doubtful that any Foulbridge Templar would be lost.

The River Derwent flows to the west of the preceptory hall. Foulbridge was the natural crossing point in medieval times; indeed, the modern crossing is only about a mile away. A few miles further west is Yedingham Priory founded sometime before 1163 by Helewise de Clere. It is now in ruins with little of the original building still standing. It was a house of Benedictine nuns and had, by all accounts, a rather 'salty' prioress at one time. It is said that there were disputes between the prioress and the Templars as to who should maintain the bridge; the story does not say who ended up providing the repairs and bearing the cost. It is interesting, though, that a prioress should stand up to the mighty Templars, considering the Templars had not been in residence very long compared to the nuns who must previously, over the years, have organised the upkeep of the bridge.

Great hall and farmhouse showing where the retaining wall of a moat may have been.

Modern pond showing possible line of moat wall.

The great hall with the long windows is on the left, while the house jutting out on the right was attached later.

The preceptory hall adjoins a Georgian farm house. For 300 years the buildings were divided into two houses, each with additions; though, for the past two and half decades, it has been lovingly restored to one homestead.

The hall is a typical medieval timber-framed building, with the trees which were used having been felled in the summer of 1288. There is some speculation that the present building stands on the foundations of an older one, but as yet, there is no proof of that. However, there are several strands of thought to play with that would suggest that there was indeed an earlier building. The land was given to the Order by Hugh Bigod who died in 1177, Henry II giving his consent for the donation to be made. The gift was later confirmed by Hugh's son, Roger. The preceptory must have been established by 1227 because further land had been donated to it by that date. The Brethren would not have camped out for all those years between being granted the original land by Hugh Bigod and the building of the preceptory whose hall still stands today. So it seems logical to suppose that a previous building existed for them to move into. Whatever the truth of the matter, it is known that the Templars employed craftsmen and artisans to do work that they could not do themselves, such as building. If necessary, they would bring them over from Europe.

The preceptory main hall is a delight and reflects the care taken in the restoration process. It is roughly 7yds wide by 15½yds long and is simply furnished, in keeping with its history. The original floor lies 18in below the present one, which was raised on the advice of a specialist architect. The arched ceiling soars about 36ft high

Interior view of the great hall from the north balcony.

General view of the great hall.

and the original rafters were reused when the roof was reduced in pitch. This has resulted in the crown plate now serving as a ridge-piece.

When it was used by the Templars, the building would have had aisles but now only the great hall survives, with a small cross wing at the north end. At some time two balconies were added, one at each end of the hall, the larger one giving access to the wing which was once used as an apple store.

The Foulbridge Brethren, as with most Templars who manned the preceptories in England, would have been over fifty years of age – considered too old to fight in the Holy Land. This didn't mean that they stayed put in the same preceptories that had admitted them to the Order. One William de Thorp had been received into the Order at Foulbridge in the first year or two of the fourteenth century; by the time the English Knights Templar were arrested in 1308, he was at Dinsley in Hertfordshire. It was not at all unusual for Brethren to travel between preceptories, nor was it unheard of for preceptors to hold office at different preceptories during the course of their Templar lifetimes.

Foulbridge Preceptory lies on the northern side of the Vale of Pickering, a valley which was a lake at one time in its very early history. Where there were once carrs, marshes and wet meadows, fertile arable land and pastures have been created through drainage systems. The area now supports canalized water courses, cuts and drainage dykes, all working to regulate the water table. This fertile area

Small cross wing at north end of the hall.

Carpenter's marks, used to show which beams should be attached to each other.

extends from the foothills of the North York Moors, south to the Yorkshire Wolds. It stretches inland from Cayton Bay and Filey for over thirty miles.

A few miles north of Foulbridge is Dalby Forest, over 8,000 acres of woodland that echoes to the sound of both bird song and pop concerts. The Forestry Commission replanted the forest in the 1920s, but it is a small area compared to the approximately 160 sq. miles that the Royal Forest of Pickering covered during Templar times. Its outer edges were Sinnington, situated halfway between Pickering and Kirkbymoorside in the west, right across to the coast in the east. Its southern boundary was the Derwent and its northern tip was at a hill not far inland from Ravenscar called Lilla Howe.

It's worth digressing for a moment to mention that one of the oldest Christian relics in England stands where the northern edge of the Royal Forest of Pickering petered out. A stone cross marks the grave of a Christian called Lilla, who was chief minister to King Edwin of Northumbria. Around AD 625, he saved the king's life, but died doing it and was buried where he fell. A quirk of fate has this ancient monument standing almost in the shadow of the very modern development of Fylingdales Early Warning System.

Medieval forest law

Although the term 'royal forest' might suggest that such areas were exclusively for the sovereign's use, this is not strictly accurate. Then, as now, forests included cultivated land and communities. Some of it was certainly the exclusive preserve of the king who relaxed by hunting there. Deer and wild boar could only be taken by the king or those who had his express permission. If land owned by local lords fell within forest boundaries, they were still subject to Forest Law. This meant that nobody could do anything without a licence from the king. Landowners needed a royal licence even to hunt such animals as hares, rabbits, foxes, wolves, badgers and wildcats on their own land. If one thinks in terms of places designated as National Parks for example, where everyday life continues as normal but what can and can't be done is tightly governed, so it was in royal forests. Pigs could forage there, but only under supervision and on payment of a fee. If the deer were fawning, the pigs weren't allowed in the forest at all. If you lived within the forest boundary you also needed a licence to keep bows and arrows and dogs or hounds. The law even went so far as to stipulate that every male above twelve years of age had to swear to observe the laws. Clergy had to observe them too, and the only time royal officers were allowed to lay hands on clerical offenders was if they broke Forest Law. Then they would appear before secular judges. This was to cause problems between Henry II and Thomas Becket, when the latter insisted that the clergy should always be tried in Church courts for any alleged crimes.

If you wanted to clear an area of forest for cultivation, you had to apply for a licence to assart – one was granted for Pickering in 1235. The work had to be meticulously carried out to ensure the land would be suitable for cultivation, as the twelfth-century Dialogue Concerning the Exchequer makes clear. In a section describing assarts, it says:

> But if groves are so cut that anyone standing still, leaning against the remaining stump of an oak, or any other tree that has been cut down, shall, on looking round, perceive five that have been cut down, they consider this a wilderness – that is, a place laid waste.

In other words, if you're going to do the job, do it properly!

From the sovereign's point of view, fines related to Forest Law offences produced huge revenue. It has to be said that the foresters who ensured the law was observed were far from popular. However unfairly, they were seen by most levels of society as tyrannical extortionists to whom innocence and justice was anathema.

The clergy & church life

The preceptory at Foulbridge had its own chapel and would have had at least one chaplain. His job was to hear confessions and give absolution. It was necessary for the Templars to have their own chaplains as this was the only member of the clergy able to perform these duties without special permission from the Pope. Members of the Order, which included the chaplains, were answerable directly to the Pope, not to local bishops and archbishops. So as well as being politically independent, the Templars were also spiritually independent.

The ordinary clergy who operated within the community were a pretty powerful bunch in medieval times, enjoying privileges which even the nobility did not share. Their right to be tried in an ecclesiastical court has already been mentioned. They were also protected from physical attack because the attacker could be excommunicated; however, it was not unknown for a priest to falsely accuse someone if it suited his purpose. They were exempt from various duties which other citizens had to undertake, such as having to accommodate passing soldiers on the march. There were also differences between their financial obligations and those of the lay person. These included being allowed to keep sufficient money for their upkeep if they got into debt. The trouble was, the amount deemed by the Church as 'sufficient money' constantly increased!

Without a doubt, there were good, honest priests who served their communities well, but they seem to have been outnumbered by those less so. Many of them, including bishops, broke ecclesiastical law by marrying and having children. Priests got drunk, swore, gambled, owned private property and slept with other men's wives. As a result, they were generally distrusted and resented, even though they were often local men.

Bishops were at the other end of the spectrum from priests and were on a par with nobility but within the Church. They were provided with both private quarters and offices in their cathedral, which was by far the largest building in a city. Archbishops and bishops were very powerful and were included in the king's council. Generally speaking, the religious hierarchy were from noble families and therefore wealthy in their own right.

By the end of the thirteenth century, there were more than 8,000 churches serving England's population of around 5 million. Medieval churches were highly decorated with paintings on the walls, paintings being a cheaper option than stained glass or statues. These paintings were put there partly for devotional purposes and partly as a method to teach or remind the congregation of stories from the Bible. Very few of these paintings have survived, but there are some beautiful fifteenth-century examples in Pickering Parish Church. Among the paintings are pictures of various saints including two very large ones of St George and St Christopher and others of John the Baptist, Edmund, St Thomas of Canterbury and St Catherine of Alexandria.

The sound of church bells would have been as familiar to medieval parishioners as they are to us today. They were used to announce the hour of church services and in monasteries they were also used to signal that one of their community was at the point of death. The oldest church bell in England with a date on is to be found in the church of St James of Compostela at Lisset near Bridlington which bears the date 1254. By that time, the practice of using church bells was very well established, dating back to the eighth century. This was also the era when two or more bells began to be found in the same church tower. They were considered to be such an essential accessory within churches that a form of blessing them was widely practised. Church bells also had some medieval superstitions attached to them. Their ringing was believed to dispel thunder and lightning, as well as calming storms at sea by scaring off the demons responsible for causing them.

There was rarely any music during church services – it's doubtful if it would have been heard above the cacophony of the congregation's chatter. Churches were considered by the peasants, who were obliged to attend Sunday services, as somewhere to catch up on the gossip as well as a place of worship. And they stood while they chatted, for there were no pews for them to use. There were seats, but these were at the front of the church and reserved for the clergy and the lord and his entourage.

Drinking occasions & ale

In addition to being used for worship and as a meeting place, churches also functioned as hospitals during epidemics. On other occasions they even had markets held inside and money-raising booze-ups outside in the grounds. At the latter function, people were encouraged to drink as much ale as possible, with single men being jollied along to imbibe until they fell down. The money raised was used to replenish the church's coffers.

If you didn't have the chance to get drunk at a church function, you could always go to the ale house. Apart from being 'the local' and therefore more easily accessible, village ale houses were a more affordable option than the large inns to be found in towns and on the main highways. Ale wasn't that cheap though, the price and standard of ale being fixed by the local authorities, as mentioned in another chapter. So a visit to the ale house would not have been a regular trip for the poorly paid labourer. Nonetheless, in the thirteenth century 'a bit of a do' was the norm to celebrate weddings, funerals and the like. As a result, rowdy behaviour was common before and during the service, as well as afterwards. This led to more than one ecclesiastical decree being issued to remind people to show more reverence during the ceremony.

There were various strengths of ale and the weaker it was, the cheaper it was. The manner of determining its strength was interesting, to say the least. The Ale Connor, who was responsible for controlling the sale of ale in a village, would sit in some of the liquid and the strength of the brew was determined by how much stuck to his leather breeches. The stickier it was, the higher its strength was considered to be. Ale was a fairly thick, sour brew and soon went off. However, ale brewed at the manor tended to be a little more palatable. Prices improved and by the fifteenth century, ale was well within the means of the lower paid.

Each year, York still honours an obligation to obey a licence and charter issued by King Henry III. It states that the sheriff of York 'has the power to punish, hear and determine all manner of felony in the city of York and the sheriff has commanded the guild to convene an assize of ale to satisfy the sheriff that the ale on sale in the city of York is of palatable quality.' This involves testing the ale in a number of pubs in the city and is used these days as a fundraiser for local charities.

Music & musical instruments

There may not have been much music inside churches, but there was certainly music to be heard elsewhere. Nor was it restricted to the minstrels' galleries in the great halls and castles. It would have been heard in all sorts of places, from the king's court to lowly ale houses.

Eleanor of Aquitaine, Henry II's wife, actively encouraged the creation of music and poetry. History books generally concentrate on her substantial political prowess, but she also inherited a family trait of enjoying and promoting music. Her grandfather was the first troubadour and her father patronised troubadours' art and poetry. When Eleanor moved to England, she continued to encourage their music, which indirectly influenced the English music scene later on.

Medieval music conjures up a romantic vision of minstrels strumming some sort of stringed instrument and singing prettily. But at the time, those same minstrels did not enjoy a very high status. They were considered to be lowly general entertainers and in addition to singing, they also juggled, danced, recited poems and played various instruments.

There was a surprisingly wide variety of instruments to play too. The shawm was a double-reed wind instrument that was the forerunner of the oboe. It was probably invented in the Middle East and it was most likely introduced into Europe around the time of the crusades. Crusaders would have been familiar with Saracen military bands whose instruments included shawms, trumpets and drums. Another wind instrument, the gemshorn, just about makes it into the Templar era as it was introduced to Britain in the early fourteenth century. It, too, has a long history and its origins go back many thousands of years to when man learned to make simple musical sounds from bones with holes in them. The gemshorn was made from an ox or goat horn and later developed into the ocarina that we are familiar with these days. It was only in use for a couple of hundred years but its name lives on, as the term is now applied to an organ stop.

Other very simple instruments were frequently played, especially by itinerant entertainers. Foremost among these would have been pipes and tabors. Another type of drum was imported from the Holy Land campaigns. It was called a naker and was certainly played by musicians in Edward I's court.

There's a wonderful image in the the Luttrell Psalter of a crowned figure playing a hand-held harp. Sir Geoffrey Luttrell was born in the late thirteenth century and lived near Grantham in Lincolnshire and the Psalter was made around 1325. These days, harps are often associated with Welsh music, but the picture in the Psalter shows that it was certainly a familiar instrument in medieval England. It is, in fact, one of the most ancient kinds of stringed instruments. At the time the Psalter was produced, the strings would usually have been made from animal gut. Another stringed instrument is one whose name we might associate with a rather different modern instrument sometimes called a barrel-organ – the hurdy-gurdy. This was a box encasing strings, with a handle to turn at one end and some keys on the outer edge. It was the first stringed instrument with a keyboard and became very popular, particularly for dance music. Then there was the equally popular rebec. This was a pear-shaped stringed instrument that used a bow and was played by resting it on the shoulder, across the chest or holding it in the armpit. It probably originated somewhere in Asia centuries before the Templars were founded. It reached Europe from the Middle East in the tenth century and was brought to England by returning crusaders – as so many things were.

Templar tenants

Once the Templars were established at Foulbridge, land and other holdings in the area which had been donated to the Order, were administered by them. For example, in 1227, Maud de Alverston (Allerston) gave them six oxgangs of land, a sizeable amount. Four years later she also gave them a mill, which would have helped increase their income. However, by 1273 this was being described as an 'empty windmill'. The modern village of Allerston, where Maud once lived, is only a few miles away from the preceptory and was home to Captain Oates who courageously left Scott's doomed Antarctic tent with the words, 'I may be some time'.

Around the same time as Maud made her donation, Alan de Monceaux gave 2 bovates with tofts in Barmston to the Knights Templar. The de Monceaux family owned most of Barmston at the time.

As mentioned earlier, the date of the preceptory's foundation is uncertain, although some authorities put it at before 1226. It is probable, however, that some tenancies listed in the 1185 Inquest fell under its jurisdiction at some stage, since they are in the vicinity. They are listed here because of that possibility:

Near Cawton of the gift of Richard Croer 1 acre which Aumund, his son, holds for 12 pennies for all services.

Near Nunnington 3 bovates of the gift of William of Stonegrave which William of Nunnington holds for 12 pennies for all services.

Near Wombleton 1 acre of the gift of Gervase which Leveric holds for 12 pennies for all services.

Near Helmsley of the gift of Walter Espic Eda 30 acres for 3 shillings for all services.

Near Scawton of the gift of Hugh Malebisse 3 bovates which Roger and his mother hold for 3s for all services.

In the same vill 2 bovates of the gift of the same Hugh which lie waste which used to pay 2 shillings.

Near Broughton of the gift of Hugh Malabisse 2 carrucates which the men of the vill hold for 40 shillings and 3 pennies, from which they owe 20 shillings rent to the same Hugh in his lifetime.

Near Ampleforth of the gift of William of Surdeval 3 acres which Everard, priest, holds for 3 shillings for all services.

Near Wilton of the gift of Ralph 1 toft which Ralph, son of Sture, holds for 16 pennies for all services.

The Inquest, or survey, of 1185 was instigated by Geoffrey Fitz Stephen, Master of England. Its object was to establish exactly what property the Order possessed and seemed to be restricted to anything which raised money for them. They gathered information on how many manors, farms, demesne lands, villages and hamlets they had. Churches and advowsons were included as were the various types of mills they ran. They also listed rents of assize and rights of common and free warren. As tenants provided the Templars with an income, as well as services, they were included in the Inquest.

Crusader imports

Earlier in this chapter there was a brief mention of the many imports the crusaders brought to British shores. Perhaps the most important were knowledge and ideas, among them science, medicine, maths, art and architecture. The crusaders also imported what might be described as more mundane items for the home, the table and the garden.

To some extent, Europeans had been aware of Arab culture and knowledge long before the crusades began. After all, the Moors had arrived in Spain and Sicily some centuries before the first crusaders started on their journey East and had made raids deep into France even earlier than that. But there remained further treasures to be found, and so returning crusaders brought more back with them than battle scars.

Medieval European physicians and surgeons are usually depicted as being considerably less skilled than their Muslim counterparts. Recent research shows this is far from being the case insofar as medical treatment by crusader doctors and surgeons is concerned. This is not to diminish the skills and knowledge of the Eastern medical professionals. There is compelling evidence of interaction between the two medical cultures, to the extent that they even worked side by side in the same hospitals. Thus when crusaders returned to England, they were able to bring further medical knowledge with them.

The crusaders introduced some useful new medicinal herbs, among them was comfrey. This later became more commonly known as 'knitbone' and 'healing herb'. Knights heading for the Holy Land used a plant from the same family for a somewhat different purpose. A sprig of borage would be put into their last drink on English soil, which was said to give them courage.

As well as introducing medicinal herbs from the East, crusaders also brought back herbs and spices for culinary use. They had developed a taste for Arabic cooking and when they returned to England, they brought coriander, basil, rosemary and ginger to help enhance the flavour of their food at home. They didn't stop at herbs and spices either. They brought back rice, coffee, sugar and a variety of fruits including apricots, melons, dates and rhubarb.

Another use of plants, apart from medicinal and culinary purposes, impressed them too. In the years between battles, they had enjoyed the gardens they had seen in the East. They brought design ideas back with them, as well as the plants necessary to emulate what they had seen. The end result was lawns and turf seats, fountains, arbours and raised flowerbeds. One of the garden plants that made the journey to England was the Apothecary Rose, perhaps better known as the Red Rose of Lancaster.

Soft soap was well known throughout Europe, but hard soap is thought to be an Arabic invention and was certainly in use by the twelfth century. The crusaders also reintroduced the personal use of perfumes, a habit which had declined after the Romans had left the country. The Arabs knew how to distil essential oils from plants to use in perfume and passed their knowledge on.

We think of people in the medieval period as being dirty; this is a long way from the truth as evidence suggests that by and large folks were quite clean. The wealthy were able to take a bath in a wooden tub, while the poorer folks strip washed and/or bathed in streams and rivers. In the larger towns, eventually, there were public baths; these continued well into the twentieth century.

Sweet smelling herbs and flowers were used to keep straw mattresses smelling sweet; added to that, fleas were kept at bay with herbs.

The era of the crusades stretched over a period of almost 200 years, but it wasn't all non-stop fighting. There was plenty of time between battles to build up trading and cultural relationships and to get to know local scholars and their work. One result was the introduction of the Arabic figures 0 to 9, making arithmetical calculations very much easier than the method in use at the time. We also learned algebra from the Saracens.

In order to help keep his new subjects in check, William the Conqueror had built castles all over the country. These were mainly wooden structures perched on top of a mound of earth, since the Roman techniques of building stone structures had been largely forgotten over the centuries. The crusaders copied the stone-built constructions they came up against in their battles and built their own versions in all the Middle Eastern countries they occupied. Edward I, having seen these substantial edifices during his tour of duty on crusade, used his knowledge to build strong castles in Wales in his efforts to subdue the Welsh. In terms of architecture, techniques such as the pointed arch, ribbed vault, and the buttress were learned from the Middle East.

And finally there was the influence of Arabic words on the English language. An *admiral* with *influenza grabs* a *guitar* while reading a *magazine* and drinking an *orange* and *lemon* squash with an ice *cube* in it – just a small selection of words in modern usage which the crusaders brought back.

7

FAXFLEET

(near Hull, c. 1185)

On a slightly raised parcel of windswept land looking seaward, and only yards from the River Humber, is the vague, visual impression of the once hugely important Faxfleet Preceptory.

The preceptory

Faxfleet was one of the most highly prized and one of the richest Templar sites in the country, not least because of its situation. The preceptory was built at some time in the twelfth century on land gifted by Roger de Mowbray in 1185. Excavations in the late 1960s revealed thirteenth-century cobbled-chalk roadways, long granaries, a brewhouse and a central hall. A 14ft wide cobbled roadway led to a circular oven, both of which were probably built by the Templars.

Faxfleet was one of only two preceptories in the whole of Great Britain which had direct access to the sea, the other being Dunwich. It is therefore reasonable to suppose that it was used by the Templars as a dock, although there is no definite evidence to support that theory. However, a royal document dated 5 September 1339 gives permission for the merchants of York to send their wool 'by little ships to Faxfleet; export duty still to be paid'. Although this is dated after the demise of the Templars, it does show that Faxfleet was a thriving shipping community at this time. In addition, from Roman times, the area had been used as a harbour for the commercial export of pottery. Add to that the local legend that there was once a small creek nearby which was used by the Templars; such an inlet would have lent itself to docking facilities, as the Blacktoft jetty just up river still does. Taking all of this together, it is reasonable to suppose that the Templars did indeed have a port at Faxfleet.

The confluence of the Rivers Trent and Ouse at the Humber estuary, connecting to the Rivers Aire and Wharfe, gave the site value and importance. This meant that the preceptories at Temple Newsam, Copmanthorpe, Wetherby and Ribston, and even those south of Faxfleet in Lincolnshire and Leicestershire could have easily sent their goods there for onward transport to continental markets and fairs and to the Middle East. River traffic would not be equalled until the arrival of the age of the canal.

The preceptory's significance was such that Edward I paid two visits to Faxfleet, once in 1302 and again in 1303. Even after the Knights Templar Order was

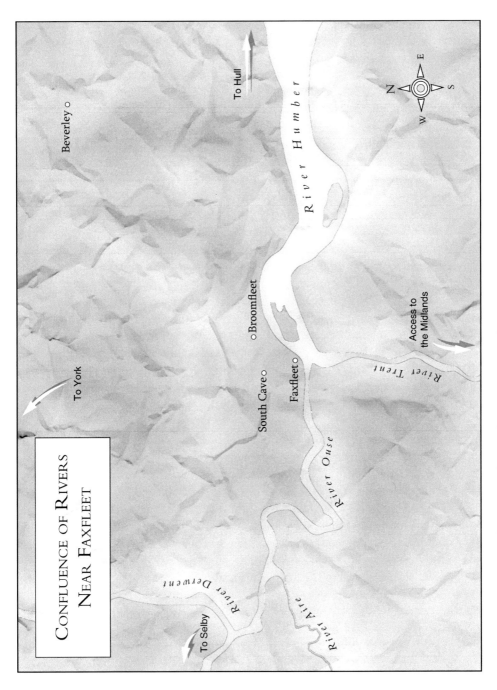

Map of the confluence of the rivers at the Humber estuary. (Jonathan Young)

dissolved, the preceptory retained its importance as shown by the fact that Edward II paid the place a visit in 1323 and Henry IV in 1407. The area on which the preceptory was built is about 11ft higher than the surrounding countryside. The deep ditches edging the modern roadsides give testimony to the need for efficient flood management. This held true during Roman and medieval times too, so there was a mastermind at work when the decision to build a preceptory in this particular location was taken.

Land reclamation & flood defences

The Domesday Book records that there were just under 6 million acres of arable land in England in 1086. By 1300 this had increased to 10.5 million acres, due in no small part to the reclamation of marshland and areas which had suffered under the 'scorched earth' policy of William the Conqueror. The early medieval landscape in Faxfleet and the surrounding area would have been salt marsh and deciduous woodland growing on a permanently wet, organic soil.

Embankment along the riverside probably began during the eleventh century. Later, in the twelfth century, medieval reclamation started and it was almost certainly continued under the direction of the Knights Templar when they arrived at Faxfleet in the thirteenth century.

Reclamation of marshland was achieved through ditching, draining and the construction of dykes and sluices. Both Edward I and Edward II commissioned reviews and repair of banks, water courses and ditches in the area. Even now, the name of Temple Dam Drain, which runs between Market Weighton and Faxfleet, is a reminder of the Order's existence here. In a way, the authorities today continue what two kings of England started, since repair work on the drain was last carried out between June 2004 and June 2006 and the pumping station was refurbished.

It was not unusual for flood defences to be jealously guarded, causing disputes with neighbours. A few miles to the northwest of Faxfleet, the inhabitants of Eastrington and Portington had dug trenches which resulted in the flooding of the adjacent area and prevented travel on the nearby common road. Worse still, people in Broomfleet and Faxfleet could not till their now sodden ground, sow seeds or graze their cattle on it. The king had to send his representatives to sort things out.

In October 1250 there was a tremendous storm in the North Sea resulting in severe flooding in large areas of England, Holland and Flanders. One has to wonder if Faxfleet's Preceptory and its tenants were saved from the worst of the floods by all the effort they had put into keeping the area well drained.

Over the centuries, the Humberside shoreline has moved further away from where the preceptory was built. However, the landscape remains as flat and uncompromising as it ever was. The plot of land where the preceptory once stood is roughly a square surrounded by a moat. The moat is clearly definable, with standing water still to be seen on two sides. At the eastern end there is evidence of a wall of faced stone together with a few blocks of stone scattered to one side. Access to the site was via a strip of land rather like a raised walkway ending at the northern edge of the moated area. There is a bit of controversy surrounding the moat as to whether it was put in by the Templars or was a later addition when in the hands of King Edward II. Records show that either the repair or the building of the moat took place in 1322. Since there were ditches and dykes of an earlier construction leading to the river, it is generally felt that the moat was constructed by the Templars. Also, the 'Close Rolls' of King Edward II show that further dykes had been repaired as part of the earthworks of the river bank that were part of the land.

Importance of Faxfleet

It has also been suggested by archaeologists that this particular preceptory may have had defensive features. Given the site, this may well be true, as attack from the riverside would have been quite possible. From the landward side, with such a flat, almost featureless landscape, there would have been, and still is, very good vision for intruders.

With the land constantly having to be drained, the bluff easterly winds buffeting across the flat, inhospitable landscape and the complicated gathering of fresh water, Faxfleet could have been seen as an outpost that Templars would not have relished working and living in. However, this could not be further from the truth. With the shipping, the nearby market at South Cave, the Templar-controlled Humber ferry and the river routes to the heart of England, it must have been an extraordinarily busy preceptory. The journey from Faxfleet to the mouth of the Humber at Hull took the time of one tide; from Faxfleet to the start of one of the upstream rivers also took one tide. So whether the sea was rolling in or the rivers rushing out, there must always have been an expectation of both large ships and small boats bringing or taking cargo. Visitors would have been many and varied with port availability. News from the East would surely have been eagerly devoured from the incoming captains and their crew. The once thriving community of Faxfleet could well have been a twenty-four hour trading post, as the tide does not halt for man's bedtime.

At Faxfleet the water was gathered by a somewhat complicated method. It was drawn from the river, but as Faxfleet was so close to the sea, water could only be drawn when the tide turned and was rolling out. Fresh river water would then be available, rather than a mix of both fresh and salt. A cullis-type gate was pulled up to allow the fresh river water to enter a dyke and from there, fill ponds both for keeping fresh water fish and for domestic use. When the tide turned once more, the gate would be lowered to keep the salt water out. It is thought that cattle were 'washed' in salt water.

There was a second reason why Faxfleet was considered to be so important to the Templars. It was a repository for deeds and records relating to the Order's substantial holdings in Scotland. Some sources also suggest that Faxfleet Preceptory held deeds and bulls for its Yorkshire property. Whether either or both of these hold true, there is no doubt that its importance is also reflected in the fact that its value in 1308 was over £290 – the most valuable preceptory in the county.

Templar tenants

The 1185 Survey shows the following tenants on Templar-controlled holdings in Faxfleet:

A mill is held by Serlo for a rent of 15 shillings.

Gille rented 2 acres for 2 shillings and 1 Monday in autumn to do 1 boonwork and 3 other boonworks and 1 hen and 10 eggs.

Serlo rented 2 acres for 20 pennies and aforesaid services.

Robert Rusel rented 2 acres for 20 pennies and aforesaid services.

Stephen rented 2 acres for 20 pennies and aforesaid services.

Harvat rented 2 acres for 20 pennies and aforesaid services.

William, son of Hardvat, rented 1 acre for 2 shillings and aforesaid services.

Richard Stubbe rented 2 acres for 20 pennies and aforesaid services.

Hugh Burre rented 2 acres for 20 pennies and aforesaid services.

Odo rented 2 acres for 20 pennies and aforesaid services.

Thomas Scrag 2 acres for 20 pennies and aforesaid services.

Ucca rented 2 acres for 20 pennies and aforesaid services.

Henry Knag rented 3 acres for 40 pennies and aforesaid services.

Stephen for fishing rights 5s for all services.

They also had property in North Cave where William of Stuteville had donated one house and grounds which Roger, son of Peter, rented from them for 12 pennies for all services.

In Drewton (with Everthorpe) Gamel held the mill of the gift of Alexander of Hibaldstow for 2½ marks for all services and for 20 shillings yearly in perpetuity. In Riplingham of the gift of Stephen one house and grounds which yielded 12 pennies. Near Broomfleet Richard held the mill for 2 marks. In Wauldby ½ carrucate of the gift of Thomas, son of Arkil, which Ralph of Beverley held for 5 shillings for all services.

And finally the most interesting of these holdings was situated near Weedley, not far from Beverley. The Inquest states that Nicholas, the son of Alexander of Hibaldstow, held a windmill for 8 shillings for all services. It is thought that this was the first post mill to be constructed in England. It has an interesting pedigree since it was certainly constructed well before the Templar Survey was carried out, and may have been built as early as 1155. Unfortunately, there's not even a village there now, only fields where people once queued to have their corn ground into flour.

The Templars continued to acquire land, property and people all over East Yorkshire long after the Survey was completed. They had a considerable amount of property in Etton near Beverley , including a grange with a chapel attached.

Markets & fairs

As mentioned earlier, the Brethren controlled a market in the area which was held at South Cave. The village is set among the low rolling hill country that marks the edge of the Wolds; today there are just 1,700 houses there. The A1034 runs through it on its way to Market Weighton and a minor road forms a junction in the middle of the village, going on past the church and winding down to the hamlet of Ellerker. These days there is a very calm and peaceful air about this lovely little village, but it would have presented a very different picture on any Monday from 1253 onwards. This was the year that Roger de Daiville assigned the weekly market to the Knights Templar, based seven miles away at Faxfleet. Daiville had been granted the market earlier by Roger de Mowbray and in 1291, Edward I confirmed the grant of the market to the Order. In May 1314, after the dissolution of the Templars, the charter was granted to Peter Dayvill, to be held at the manor. As was often the case when the Order charged for anything, they were accused of taking excessive tolls at South Cave market, which continued to be held until 1939.

The right to hold a market was a privilege granted by the king to those nobles who had served him well. They, in turn, assigned those rights to their own favoured people. The grant at South Cave was for a prescriptive market, which meant that it had to either have a mint or be a borough. South Cave certainly did not have a mint, but it was a borough. Not all towns were recognised as boroughs though; this status was granted to a town and involved a precise set of privileges, which varied from one town to another.

It was the general practice in markets to allow local inhabitants to have the best positions, but if traders were coming from outside the town with fresh provisions, they were also favoured. Health inspectors are no modern development; in medieval times they watched out for the safe disposal of rotting goods after the market, since, apart from the smell being offensive, pollution could spoil agricultural ground. It was also part of their job to ensure that the pies on sale had been freshly cooked and were not just reheated old stock. Another check carried out by officials was on weights and measures.

A fair was also held every year in South Cave on the Feast of Holy Trinity, and was certainly still being held in the sixteenth century. It too was prescriptive. Although the actual fair lasted one day, normal practice was to carry fairs on for four days. Day one would be a vigil, day two would be the actual day of the fair and the next two days were also considered to be part of fair time. Even though everyone would normally have to attend church on feast days as well as Sundays, anyone who sold goods at the fair was excused from going to church.

Birds

At Faxfleet one can still climb up onto the river embankment and walk the path leading to Blacktoft Sands which is now a protected bird sanctuary. The air is moist as it always has been, with birds swooping and diving, untroubled in their search for food across the expanse of reed beds and salt marsh. A huge fish pond dips down away from the river producing a tranquil scene for the walker.

Over 270 species of bird have been recorded on the reserve, some of which would have been known to the Templars, though others would not. They would also have been familiar with some birds which we would be surprised to find existed on the marshlands near Faxfleet Preceptory. One of those was the fourth largest eagle in the world – the White-Tailed Sea Eagle. Although they are to be found across Europe and in parts of Asia, they were on the verge of extinction in this country until they were reintroduced in Scotland in the 1970s, though their numbers are still low. Spoonbills have been seen recently at the RSPB site, and they would have been familiar to the Templars, as would Marsh Harriers and swans – both of which can still be seen there. But they would not have recognised the ubiquitous Canada Goose, which did not arrive in this country until the late seventeenth century.

It's worth mentioning that swans, cranes, waders and herons all ended up on the medieval banqueting table, and one has to wonder if they also found their way into the kitchen at Faxfleet Preceptory.

Two knights' effigies

Five miles east of Faxfleet as the crow flies is the village of Welton. There, in St Helen's Church, lies the recumbent figure of a knight, locally believed to be that of a Knight Templar. It is, however, more likely to be someone who was simply an associate member of the Order, since their vows of poverty precluded Knights Templar from having effigies on their graves. Associates joined for a specific length of time and generally made a donation for the privilege of doing so.

St Helen's Church, Welton, where the knight's effigy lies.

The Welton knight.

   The Purbeck marble figure dates from about 1250–1275; effigies in Purbeck marble are rare and the Welton knight is the most northerly example known. Brought by sea from Dorset, the material is expensive and denotes the knight to be a man of substance and importance. As an aside, Purbeck marble is used extensively as column shafts in both Beverly and York Minster which conveys the riches poured into these two cathedrals. The nearest preceptory to Welton is Faxfleet, where it is

All Saint's Church, Routh, where another knight's effigy lies.

presumed the knight would have had close associations. The knight had originally been in an upright position but now lies horizontally. Patterns remain on the sword, the lower leg and on the left side. Purbeck marble does not wear as well as stone and deteriorates quickly when left outside, which may have happened with this effigy.

Unfortunately the knight was defaced during an uprising around 1830. This may have had something to do with a general uprising among the working classes for an increase of wages by the labouring men of the parish. The enclosures of 1770–1830 had been the catalyst for the Tolpuddle Martyrs' action and unrest had been festering throughout the countryside at this time.

Another interesting tomb is to be found at Routh, to the north-east of Beverley. There has been a community at Routh for over 1,000 years, with the earliest record found in the Domesday Book. Richard de Scruteville built the first church in the late twelfth century. During the fourteenth century, the present church was built and dedicated to All Saints. The church is situated part way along Meaux Lane, which eventually leads to the destroyed Abbey of Meaux. The abbey was closed in 1539 during the dissolution of the monasteries by King Henry VIII. When the abbey was demolished, the stones were used to build town defences for Kingston-upon-Hull which, in the past, had close associations with Meaux Abbey.

The knight here, however, has not been positively identified as a Knight Templar. In better shape than the one at Welton and in similar repose, the effigy is made of stone which is slightly defaced around the head. He lies in a dark corner of the sanctuary close to the altar by the north wall. The tombstone is believed to be from the grave of Sir William de Routh, buried in the earlier church in 1240. If he was indeed a Knight Templar, then he also would have had associations with Faxfleet Preceptory.

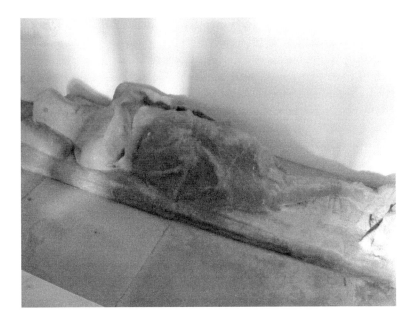

The Routh knight.

Sea travel & ships

The ocean has always held a fascination for man and has been a vehicle for his travels since time began. Piracy is just as old, dating from the time of the ancient Greeks to the Romans, a golden time for piracy, and the Vikings. Piracy is thousands of years old and continues to this day. The earliest known record of piracy was in the Aegean Sea during the thirteenth century BC!

The Knights Templar, along with other fighting orders, would have been very familiar with fighting Muslims on the high seas, as well as on land during the crusades. Both Christian and Muslim pirates were very skilled seaman and the booty they acquired included passengers and crew, as well the cargo. Rich passengers would be held for ransom, while others would be sold as slaves or used as crew. Even after the fall of Acre in 1291, the Knights Templar, together with other orders such as the Knights Hospitaller, continued to harass Muslim ships. It was through the crusades that shipping, and therefore piracy, saw a resurgence.

The Venetians and Genoese, the great sea rivals of the time, employed corsair captains to territorialise their waterways in an attempt to help counter piracy. This, in a sense, was a similar *raison d'être* as the Hanseatic League which was established about 1158 to stop the scourge of raids and piracy prevalent in the Baltic and North Seas since the age of the Vikings.

The islands of Sardinia, Crete, Cyprus, Rhodes and Malta have all, at times, played a crucial part in controlling the high Mediterranean Sea. Corsairs of various nations preyed on countries with which hostilities were rife and sometimes even countries with which they held allegiances.

Apart from the order to guard territorial waters, the corsairs were also expected to enforce the limits set by European countries on commercial merchandise. Significant leeway was used by the captains in this, and often the accepted mark was overstepped. The boundary between enforcement and piracy proved to be very thin. Over 750 cases of arbitration are recorded at various courts throughout Europe from about 1200 to 1400.

While some captains were fair, others were very cruel and just plain outlaws. Many seamen were serving on ships because there was no other way for them to earn a living, but their life was hard. The power of the captain was absolute. Some exercised discretion; others would order a whipping for the slightest misdemeanour by a crewman. Having said this, many ships were run in a very democratic fashion. Before an expedition was undertaken, a meeting took place that included all crew members. Various decisions would be taken such as how the booty would be divided, those with special skills such as a carpenter getting a larger cut. Rules were also determined to which everyone signed up.

Maps were rare in medieval times, and charts of the seas were rarer. However, there were papers called portulan charts which served as a system for merchant shipping navigation. There are indications that the earliest chart was drawn up for a Genoese admiral, Benedetto Zaccaria.

The early portulan charts were prepared on vellum made from either sheep or goatskin. They were drawn using a network of directional lines radiating out from a compass rose. Features commonly included place names crowded along the shoreline, together with flags and banners of different cities.

The suffix 'rose' of the compass arises from ornate figures used with early compasses; for instance a fleur-de-lis evolved from the letter T in the north wind's name 'Tramontane', often used to indicate the direction north. Similarly, on these old maps, L for 'Levante' was used to indicate the direction of Jerusalem as seen from the view of Western Europe. From some time in the Middle Ages, map makers changed from a 12-point rose to a 16-point rose, arguing that sailors were no longer educated enough to understand the original 12-point at 30 degree rose used by the Romans.

The name portulan is taken from written sailing directions, 'portolani'. The portulan maps were, in the early days, centred on the Mediterranean Sea. Thus, the Mediterranean became a waterway artery with an accord between corsairs and merchant vessels. By 1354, King Peter the Ceremonious of Catalan-Aragon ordered that every ship armed for naval warfare should have at least two portulan charts.

The sea now gave a freedom of movement which allowed captains to overcome the political antagonism that separated territorial space. Corsairs and merchants were involved in privateering – legal piracy on the high seas. The world held a different shape than on land. That sea was not bound together by the tight Christian belief of Western Europe, but rather by the rivalries of Europe. An agenda by the purveyors of sea theft was for the exploitation of any and every vessel. The sea became a connective link; cultural and political alliances developed that simply would not have happened on home territory.

An interesting seafaring personality of the time was Roger de Flor, who was almost certainly a sergeant for the Templar fleet and is thought to have maybe become a captain of the Templar ship, the *Falcon*. What we do know is that in May 1291, de Flor was instrumental in helping the affluent society escape from Acre; the downside is that he also helped himself to their wealth. He was also accused of keeping much of the merchandise plundered from other ships which should have gone to the Templar cause. The Grand Master, Jaques de Molay expelled him from the Order and he fled to Marseilles where he became a very successful, if infamous, privateer. It is thought that he still kept contact with some Templars. He may have acted as a spy, providing much needed intelligence for them. He later married into an influential Byzantine family and created his own navy from disaffected soldiers. He harried the Turks working for Andonkios, the Byzantine emperor, but alas, he was stabbed to death in 1305. Some believe that the Pope and King Philip of France would not have made a move against the Knights Templar had de Flor not been murdered. He had a network of informers across Europe and would have known of any moves made against the Order. The implications of de Flor's death and the circumstances surrounding it are an endless source of speculation.

At some time during the height of the crusades, a vessel was developed from the common ship design. It could be seen as forerunner of the 'roll on roll off' ferries of today. Most of the war horses appeared to have been trained in France and a good deal of travel to the Holy Land could be completed on land. However, there were

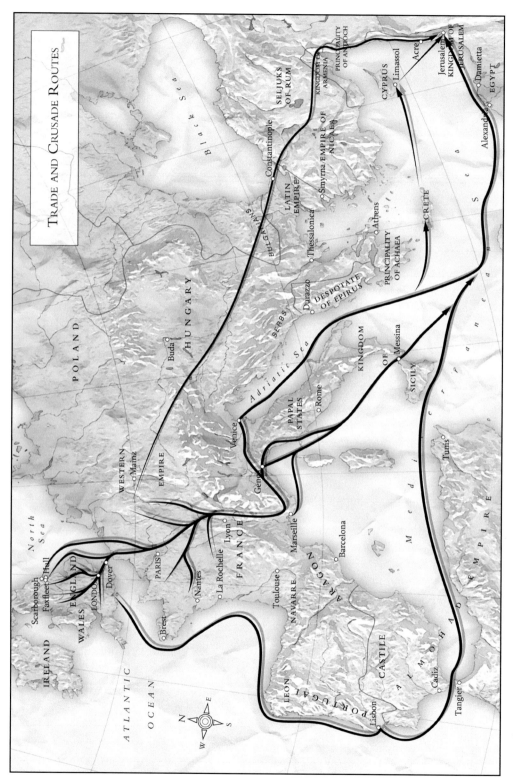

Map of trade and pilgrim routes to the Holy Land.

instances when the horses had to travel by sea. To this end, some Templar ships had a bow which could be opened and let down for the horses to enter and exit the boat. The trained war horses were an expensive commodity and needed to be well looked after on any sea voyage; therefore, the development of such a design to allow the horses a comfortable ascent and descent from the ship was imperative. There were also special horse transporters called tarides, which would be towed behind the galleys.

By about 1290, the great galley ships were launched; they were up to 150ft in length, 200 men to crew with oarsmen armed, together with up to thirty bowmen. The Templar Order became known for its logistical achievements with a fleet of some fifty ships. So good were they at delivering their cargo, be that people or goods, that France, in particular, restricted the number of pilgrims they were allowed to carry to the Holy Land.

The following quote is from a collection of French chronicles called the *Gestes des Chiprois*: ' In 1279 the Master of the Temple armed 13 galleys and sent them to Jubail. Several Brethren came on shore . . . Then the galleys of the Templars came up outside Tripoli where, as it happened they encountered bad weather and three of them ran aground.' It is possible that some ships were hired by the Templars as owning so many would have proved most expensive, although there is evidence that they also built their own ships in Acre and La Rochelle. Ships were also hired by various kings and dignitaries, as a standing navy was not kept at that time.

Apart from transporting horses, Templar ships also played a crucial part in moving goods, money and essential supplies, including cheese and mead to the East. The ships would return with, among other things, spices and almonds, used at this time as a sweetener in cooking and as a substitute for milk after the almonds had had a long soaking. Papers, coin and important personnel were entrusted to the Templar ships, which were much more reliable than others. There are shipping records from La Rochelle showing that the Templars were exporting wine from France. Though records are thin on the ground, it is most likely that Templar ships carried other types of produce from England such as wool, tanned skins and pack animals.

This brings us back to Faxfleet and the part it played in the export of goods from England. As mentioned earlier, it was one of only two preceptories in Britain that had direct access to the sea. There was a preceptory at Dover, but it was situated inland, not on the coast itself.

North Ferriby

This whole area has a long history of seamanship. Nearby North Ferriby is a place with a long tradition of a safe ferry crossing. Part of a boat carbon dated as far back as 2030–1780 BC shows that the area had been in use as a crossing and for boat building for over 4,000 years. The Templars, during their time at Faxfleet, had the right of charging for crossing the river at this point. Yet again, they were accused of demanding too much for the facility. A ferry continued to exist here until the Humber Bridge was completed in June 1981.

There are occasional references in various nineteenth-century books and notes to a Knights Templar priory at North Ferriby, said to have been founded in the twelfth century by Lord Eustace de Vesci. The de Vesci family did indeed found a priory at North Ferriby in 1152, but it was not for the Knights Templar. There was a little known religious order with the title 'The House of the Lord's Temple of Jerusalem' and its only priory in England was the one founded for them at North Ferriby. The full title of the Knights Templar was 'The Order of the Poor Knights of Christ of the Temple of Solomon in Jerusalem'. It would seem that Victorian writers homed in on the words 'Temple' and 'Jerusalem', jumped to the wrong conclusion and, one after another, perpetuated incorrect information.

Blacktoft

The demise of Faxfleet is not easy to understand. When the dissolution of the Templars came about, it would be reasonable to expect Faxfleet to have maintained itself as a route to Europe, even with the cessation of the crusades. However, this was not to be. Nearby Blacktoft is still a thriving, albeit small community with a public house; an earlier pub, the Bay Horse Inn, was situated opposite the jetty. It also has a church, Holy Trinity of St Clement, dating from about 1070. It exists because of the conversion to Christianity of William de Blaketoft, believed to be the great-great-grandson of the community's founder, Blake. Proof of the existence of an earlier stone church is exhibited in a tombstone from the period 1125–75. As with many such small communities, the nave has variously been used as a school, a market hall and for other social and community events, as well as for worship.

Broomfleet

Broomfleet, a couple of miles away, was also a thriving community at the time of the Templars and continues to be so. The difference is this; Broomfleet was under the auspices of St Leonard's Hospital in York. The hospital is thought to have been founded by King Athelstan in about 936; subsequently, claims were also made by both William the Conqueror and his son, Rufus, to the founding of the hospital. It was called St Peter's to avoid confusion with nearby York Minster. What we do know is that King Stephen moved the hospital westward and constructed a church dedicated to St Leonard; thus the hospital became known by the same name and was staffed by a group of Brethren and Sisters leading an ecclesiastical lifestyle, plus laymen. The hospital accrued widespread land in order to finance its costs. Not all was sweetness and light for the hospital though. It had access to St Leonard's Landing on the riverside, giving it special privileges within the city of York, such as trade advantages, which had the effect of alienating the local traders and merchants. In this they were similar to the Knights Templar with their special trade benefits. The Hospital continued until the time of the Dissolution, lasting over 400 years, but fell into disrepair and subsequently, financial ruin. But Broomfleet by this time was in a strong position and maintained itself as a thriving community. There have been times when there have been less than 100 inhabitants, but it now flourishes with St Mary's Church, a pub, shops and modern housing sitting easily alongside older houses and farms.

The demise of Faxfleet

Faxfleet, however, fell into disuse, without an overarching administrator and the eventual loss of patronage by the king. This patronage is seen through the king's clerks appointed to oversee the parish and to ensure the church was provided with a priest. The Crown held Faxfleet only until 1326 and the royal connection ended when, in 1391, there was a dispute over the tithes and taxes with Warden Pygot. The dispute went in favour of the mother church. The chaplaincy was no longer worth having and Faxfleet was not established as a separate parish. Then Hull gradually took over as the major port and this seems finally to have marked the demise of Faxfleet as a thriving community.

Boats still ply the River Humber and on into the Trent and Ouse, hardly noticing as they pass the small hamlet of Faxfleet.

8

WESTERDALE

(near Whitby, c. 1203)

Westerdale straddles the Westerdale Moor; the dale is so called because it is the most westerly of the Esk valley dales. One of the little Esklets (a stream that joins the Esk River) bubbles alongside where the Templar preceptory once stood. The young River Esk rises and briskly runs along at the base of the village where a ford is still the only way of crossing from the moorland into the village, though a lovely old packhorse bridge is still standing a few yards further on. The late thirteenth-century bridge was restored in 1874 and spans the River Esk on a single, segmental arch. The bridge now just leads from the lane into a field which suggests the route to the village has changed; possibly a 'new' road was built at some point.

Packhorse bridge over the River Esk near Westerdale.

There are only about twenty houses plus a number of scattered farms now – a reliable informant in the shape of a pretty young girl says that there are only fifteen children in the area and they all have to travel on a bus to Castleton to go to school.

Ralf's cross

The village is surrounded by rough, broken moorland and one moves rapidly downhill from the moor into the village and almost immediately, the climb up and out begins. The highest point is at Ralf's cross at 1,407ft heading towards Whitby and to the south-west Stony Ridge at 1,424ft. The reason for the cross has long since been lost, together with just who Ralf was. Baysdale Abbey, to the west of Westerdale, was once well known for purebred shorthorn cattle; a Cistercian nunnery moved there during the reign of King Henry II. Originally, the nunnery had been sited at the head of the valley; it then moved to Nunthorpe and finally to Baysdale and was founded by Ralf de Neville in about the twelfth century. One must wonder if there is any connection to the Ralf's cross!

The preceptory

Nearby, at Stockdale beck there are still fragments of ancient woodland which the Templars would have had knowledge of, though it was probably not in their hands.

Despite its isolated location, the Westerdale upland has been farmed for many, many hundreds of years, and the resident Templars at Westerdale Preceptory would still feel they were in very familiar surroundings.

A Ralf's cross near Westerdale.

The preceptory stood at the base of a small hill, which is different from other Templar sites in Yorkshire as most of them sit on raised ground. The remains of the Templar preceptory had been excavated in 1960 and evidence was found of a main chamber, a kitchen, a brewery and a chapel. Cobbled roadways were found dating from the earliest occupation by the Templars, together with a coin that dated to about the mid-thirteenth century. Animal quarters were also found. The site of the preceptory lies behind Westerdale Hall, designed by Thomas H. Wyatt as a shooting lodge; later, after the Second World War, it became a youth hostel. The hall is once again a private residence and is a very gothic looking structure, though modernisation can be seen which is not always sympathetic to the building. Nevertheless, it looks like a delightful building in an atmospheric setting.

Quite a number of ancient crosses and marker stones are to be seen on the moor, some of which may have marked the boundary of the Templars' lands, and some even predate their era. However, stone crosses and stone markers were used extensively by both the Knights Templar and the Hospitallers to maintain their boundaries and to prevent disputes. To the north of the preceptory is a site of tumuli which may also have been used as a boundary marker.

The village would have been a hive of industry then, rather than the sleepy village of today. It appears that the Knights Templar held the whole of Westerdale township, from about 1203 on land donated by Guido de Bovingcourt. Among the tradespeople in the village, there would have been a wheelwright, blacksmith and miller plus all the people working on the Templar site. Even by the eighteenth century, many of these trades were still in existence plus a few more such as a shop owner, two shoemakers, a teacher and in the region of fourteen farms. With a church and a school, the area supported a strong community.

Iron smelting

To the east, there is evidence of a bloomery, a type of furnace used for smelting iron. The bloomery was the earliest form of a smelter which consisted of a pit with heat-resistant walls made of clay or stone. Close to the base, clay pipes went through the wall to allow air to filter in to permit a natural draft through the furnace to allow for the maintenance of the heat; bellows could be inserted to provide additional air flow.

One reason why the Knights Templar may have decided to build a preceptory in this remote location was the ready supply of iron ore nearby. Whether they built the bloomery or whether it was already there is unknown. But the blacksmith would certainly have had a good supply of material to work with and plenty of work to do.

Blacksmiths

Blacksmithing is an ancient craft and was absolutely vital during the Middle Ages. There were forges at manors, in towns and at Templar preceptories. There were travelling blacksmiths who plied their trade to those who couldn't afford to employ one of their own. As well as making tools, knives, cooking utensils and horse shoes, they made chain-mail ('mail' meaning hammered), weapons and armour. In addition to practical items, they also produced some very artistic work which can still be seen in twelfth- and thirteenth-century churches.

The wool economy

There are many various types of soils across the dale, from loose draining shale to cloggy clay. The dale has historically been used for arable crops, with farming features dating from the Bronze and Iron Age as well as it being a strong sheep rearing area. So, one way or another, crops, sheep and cattle have been part of the Westerdale landscape.

Wool underpinned the English economy for many generations. The real boom period in medieval England were the thirteenth and early fourteenth centuries and Yorkshire was very much a part of it all. Henry de Lacy, for example, kept almost 7,000 sheep on his lands in Yorkshire and Lincolnshire and as many again in the South of England. Despite widespread outbreaks of disease in sheep, wool exports nonetheless increased during the reigns of Edward I and Edward II.

Recognising a good thing when he saw it, in 1297, Edward I decided that the high taxes on wool exports granted in 1294 be granted to him again. Despite the clear violation of Magna Carta, which stated that taxes had to be agreed by the

Recovered farmland near Westerdale Preceptory.

great landowners together with representatives of the knights and commons, he went ahead with imposing this tax. He was checked, though, by being made to sign the 'Confirmation of Charters'. This meant that the monarch could no longer impose taxes as and when he saw fit, but needed Parliament's approval.

The first customs duty on wool had been introduced in 1275 and was an export tax which was referred to as the 'Ancient Custom', even though it was a new tax. A charge was made of 6s 8d per sack. In 1303 a further tax of 3s 4d per sack was imposed on foreign exporters in addition to that already charged, known as the 'New Custom' or 'Petty Custom'. As usual, the Templars were exempt from all of it. The reasoning behind this additional tax on foreign entrepreneurs can be understood when realised that the greater part of the wool export business was in the hands of foreigners.

Along with the Cistercians, the Knights Templar saw the economic potential in the wool trade and used it to their advantage. It is known that the monasteries dealt in 'futures' and sold the wool they expected to have in two or three years time – sometimes even fifteen – twenty years ahead! So this type of trading is not a new phenomenon by any means. The Cistercians forbade their monasteries to trade in this way, but many individual monasteries took no notice and continued doing it.

The Templars were quite often given land that the Cistercians thought that they themselves should have had, so frequently, there was bad feeling between the two orders. This did not, however, seem to extend to caring for their flocks. The Templars had granted Byland Abbey some pasture land near Thirsk where the Cistercians had, in fact, already made an enclosure close to their sheep-fold. It was agreed that if sheep belonging to Templar tenants should stray into that enclosure, the animals were not to be harmed, but driven back.

Wool left Yorkshire's shores from two ports – possibly three if Faxfleet really had its own harbour. One of the ports was Hull, which came into existence in the twelfth century when monks from the local Meaux Abbey found themselves in need of a port from which they could export their wool to the Continent. Trading was certainly established by 1198 when forty-five sacks of wool were sold from the town and by 1205, Hull ranked sixth in importance as an English port. Scarborough was also used to export wool. In 1225, Henry III gave Scarborough the right to levy tolls on boats, ships and carts, which was a nice little earner for them which helped pay the cost of building and maintaining their harbour and quays, among other things. Customs officials there, as at all English ports, were expected to record everything in very great detail.

On the receiving end of these sacks of wool were the Italians, who made cloth from it, and Flanders, which almost totally depended on this import for their economic survival. So much so, that when the wool failed to get through to them in 1297, Flanders was 'well nigh empty because the people cannot have the wools of England', according to the English chronicler, Heminburgh. The resulting widespread unemployment had dire results, causing terrible starvation among the population that year.

Although the monasteries are generally thought of as being the main suppliers of medieval wool, the peasantry also often kept one or two sheep each and added their fleeces to the total exports. Some commentators suggest that the wool supplied countrywide by these local individuals exceeded the amount provided by all the monastic houses together.

At Pontefract and Pickering, stock-keepers were employed whose responsibility it was to collect the wool from the various manors in the area. Their duties also included buying and selling sheep. The job of actually looking after the flocks fell to the shepherd, but it wasn't quite as lowly a job as one might imagine. For a start, he wasn't expected to take part in the washing and shearing; that job was undertaken by tenants as part of their boonwork. He also benefited from certain rights and privileges, some of which went right back to Anglo-Saxon times. He could have bowls of whey all year and ewe's milk on Sundays. He could choose a lamb at weaning time and a fleece when the sheep were sheared. He was allowed to keep his own sheep with the lord's flock, which meant his animals enjoyed the same good pastures as his master's. For a fortnight at Christmas he was allowed to keep the entire flock on his own land. This may not sound like much of a benefit until one takes into account that he also got all the manure the sheep produced, which he could use to improve his own land.

The sheep he cared for would have been smaller than those we see today. Bones found during archaeological digs seem to indicate that the animals were also slender. Some sheep skulls were found at Kirkstall Abbey which were thought may have been from hairy Pennine hill sheep. Some skulls were horned and others were not and it was thought that the hornless skulls may have indicated long-wool sheep. On the other hand, they could equally well have been the skulls of horned rams and hornless ewes. There was no way to be sure. Sheep from different parts of the country produced different types of wool; smaller sheep had short wool, while larger ones produced longer wool. We know for certain that Yorkshire wool was much sought after and that foreign wool merchants made a point of visiting the county to buy it. They also bought wool from Lincolnshire, whose wool was the finer of the two counties.

At that time sheep were bred purely for their wool, not for meat. The only time they were eaten was if their wool was no good or if for some reason they weren't good breeding stock.

The grain economy

As mentioned earlier in this chapter, Westerdale has had a long history of growing arable crops which would have included cereal crops. While the peasantry made a strong contribution to the wool trade, they did little to help the grain economy. After feeding themselves, keeping seed for the following year and giving their tithe to the local church, there was very little left over to sell directly. Strictly speaking, some of their crops would have reached the markets, but only through the local church which would have collected one tenth of their yield from them and sold it on.

Most of the grain which found its way to market came from the manors, churches and monasteries. Tithes were a very important source of income to the Church; for example, between 1305 and 1319, sixty-five per cent of Bolton Priory's income came from the sale of corn paid to it through tithes. Bearing in mind the number of people any monastery had to feed, that was no mean achievement. A large percentage of the crops grown on manors would have been sold and it's not unreasonable to suppose that that would also have applied to what was grown by the Templars and their tenants at Westerdale.

Some of the customers were to be found in local towns, where people had no land to grow anything. They bought what they needed from markets to use, both for their own consumption and to feed their horses. They would have either bought directly from the producers or from cooks and bakers. River transport was often used to get the grain where it was supposed to go, but surprisingly, it also frequently went by boat along the coast.

Grain, mostly made up of wheat, was also an important export, being shipped abroad to the Low Countries. As with wool, the merchants who handled it were mostly foreigners. For the twelve-month period from July 1304, the grain they exported from Hull made up fifty-three per cent of the value of goods passing through the port.

The king had the right to buy grain by compulsory purchase and Yorkshire was on the receiving end of this right under Edward I. He needed to feed his troops and horses on his frequent forays into Scotland, while Yorkshire, along with some of the other eastern counties, had to supply him.

Monasteries

Monasteries, which contributed so much to the economy of the time, were an integral part of life in the Middle Ages, with some beautiful buildings still to be seen across the country.

The oldest known monastic order was in Egypt where Christians lived alone, but gathered to pray as a community in chapels. This was not an order that we recognise today but was a move forward from the retiring early Essenes, the first recorded community of holy men and women. St Anthony's Monastery claims the title of the oldest inhabited monastery in the world. It is reputed to have been built in the mid-fourth century over the tomb of St Anthony, and is deep in the Red Sea Mountains, still relying on natural springs for water. The rituals have barely changed in sixteen centuries.

St Catherine's is a famous monastery in Sinai and stems from the Greek Orthodox Christian Church. It is considered a defining feature of the Holy Land and people have worshipped there for fifteen centuries.

The Benedictine Rule was the first monastery to be established in England at Canterbury when St Augustine arrived around AD 597. In the latter part of the eleventh century other, monasteries materialised, the most important being the Cistercians. These were an austere sect and their Rule kept them in seclusion. Other monastic orders included the Augustinians, Cluniacs and the Brigittines.

Some of the large monasteries such as Fountains Abbey in North Yorkshire could accommodate up to a thousand monks. These places were small economic communities in their own right.

Yorkshire has a plethora of abbeys and monasteries, the remains of which remind us of the debt we owe to the monks for their industrious work ethic. Some, such as Whitby Abbey, were in existence long before the arrival of William the Conqueror, while others were relative latecomers like the Carthusians, which in England was called the Charterhouse. At Staddle Bridge in North Yorkshire, the Charterhouse Priory of Mount Grace has the finest remains of the ten founded in Britain. Above the hillside of Mount Grace Priory is the chapel of Our Lady of Grace; this was an outlying chapel of the monks and is a well-known site for pilgrims. Though fairly near to the busy A19 and only a stone's throw from the Cleveland way walk, nevertheless, it retains a feeling of total isolation and has an atmospheric air about it. It is now administered by the Benedictine monks from the nearby abbey at Osmotherley; they hold regular services and it is a thriving religious centre.

Thanks to monks of every order, we have very good records, not only of the Middle Ages, but also of major ancient texts. They beavered away in their libraries and cells and left us a priceless legacy of manuscripts.

Templar tenants

Westerdale was founded after the 1185 survey had been carried out. There are a number of tenancies which may have belonged to Temple Cowton but because of their location, perhaps they were administered by Westerdale later on. There's no way to be sure as the tenancies are all listed under 'Kirby', the modern Cold Kirby. However, for interest, a few of them are shown here; the going rate for rent seemed to average at 20 pennies per bovate.

Near (Cold) Kirby of the gift of Richard Croer 6 carrucates;

Theodric 10 bovates for a rent of 16 shillings and 8 pennies and 2 assarts for no service.

Ralph, son of Tancard 2 bovates for a rent of 40 pennies for all services.

Utting, son of Grimkel, 1 bovate for a rent of 20 pennies for all services.

Gamel, son of Hucca, 1 bovate for a rent of 20 pennies for all services.

Waltheof, son of Hucca, 1 bovate for a rent of 20 pennies for all services.

William, son of Tancard, 2 bovates for a rent of 40 pennies for all services.

Robert, son of Ouca, 3 acres for a rent of 15 pennies for all services.

Also Theodric 3 acres for a rent of 15 pennies which he has in guardianship with Eda, his daughter, for his grandson.

---

30 acres are in demesne, by agreement with the men may be more, (for) which they have to give 16 shillings. The men of Kirby say of their oath that if all agree that it is not possible to finish because of the brothers, they shall have half the forfeit and the brothers the other half, and if through their own fault, the brothers will have all the forfeit, and they will give for their obit a third part. [An obit was a note recording a death. Obits were often entered into liturgical calendars to commemorate the deceased.]

9

RIBSTON WITH WETHERBY

(near and in Wetherby, c. 1217)

The preceptory

The preceptory at Ribston was founded in 1217 and seems to have originated from a gift of land by Robert de Ros. This included a manor, vill and mill at Ribston, together with the advowson of the church at Walshford and the vill of Hunsingore, all inherited from de Ros' mother, Rose Trussebut. At some time before 1240, his maternal aunts, Hilary and Agatha, granted the Templars various woods near the preceptory. At its height, Ribston comprised more than 900 acres of arable land, 30 acres of meadow and four water mills. Added to this there were a number of rents, fees and perquisites of the manor court. In addition to this, the Templars acquired further lands and manors at Sicklinghall, Cowthorpe and Cattal, all local to Ribston, plus Ilkley, much further away.

Wetherby nestles at the western edge of the Vale of York, close to the River Wharfe, which at the time of the Templars, formed the southern extremity. Wetherby is now a successful market town and rivals nearby historic Knaresborough. One of the successes of the town is the racecourse which now borders the far side of the A1 motorway. The first ever horse-racing at Wetherby, and indeed in England, is attributed to the Roman Emperor, Severus (AD 146–211). It is claimed that a Roman legion stationed there 'ran some horse races for the delectation of the Emperor Severus'. It is nice to think that so long a tradition still boasts such a strong connection.

The town boasts a long history which goes well beyond its 750 year anniversary celebrated a few years ago. Prior to that time, Wetherby etched its early development into the edge of the River Wharfe, even before the beginning of the Roman occupation. The Wharfe was, and still is, a dangerous river to cross and Wetherby grew up because of the ford at this point in river.

Spofforth

When the Normans invaded England, the north did not give up easily; after 1069, William, having subdued his belligerent northern subjects, divided up the Yorkshire area between various nobles. Wetherby was, in the early stages of William's reign, held by the great Percy family, later to become the mighty and influential dukes of Northumberland. It is thought that it was they, rather than William the Conqueror, who were responsible for building the castle at Wetherby to guard the river crossing. The castle building cannot be dated with any surety, but the best guess is that it was built early in the twelfth century. All that is left are the foundations of the keep, about 57sq.ft, with the walls being about 15ft thick. By 1133, the fourth Baron Percy held many estates throughout Yorkshire and Lincolnshire. Spofforth was one of their main seats due to the iron industry they owned there. For a while, Spofforth assumed an importance out of proportion to its size. It took on an extra parochial role and in 1224 the vill was granted a licence by King Henry III for a Friday market which has since died out. The Percy family also built a castle there and the ruins of a later fortified manor can still be visited. The castle ruins are still owned by a descendent of the Percy family, the Earl of Egrement, so a long history of association still exists.

Many readers will have heard of Harry Hotspur which was a nickname for Sir Henry Percy whose birthplace was Spofforth Castle; he was immortalised through the Shakespeare plays of *Richard II* and *Henry IV*. Clearly Shakespeare took liberties with changing his age but then, the plays were works of fiction.

Spofforth Church is dedicated to All Saints and worshippers have been able to express their reverence and devotion to God for over a thousand years. The church carries a reminder of a foregone age. At the eastern end of the church there is a Templar cross carved into a stone. The stone looks relatively new, so whether it is a replacement or an addition is not known.

Spofforth Castle ruins.

Gifts to the Order

Wetherby was quite an insignificant place for the family in terms of output, the river crossing being the single noteworthy acquisition. The Percys held many villages in the area but today Wetherby outshines them all in terms of importance; it still has a thriving market and is a flourishing township.

The first known gift to the Templars in Wetherby was in 1238; this was the bequest of William de Denby, son of Robert. He granted a mill, 38 bovates and 90 acres of land in Wetherby. A second grant by William of 17 bovates completed the axing of the fee of Wetherby held by the Denbys. Apart from the Denbys, who appear to be under-tenants, further grants were made to the Templars in 1240, 1246 and 1248 which amounted to free warren in the demesne lands of the manor of Wetherby and yet more land in 1284 and 1290. The Percys continued as tenants-in-chief for the king. The 1276 inquisition records that the Templars held 3 carucates of land in Wetherby from the Percy fee, which had been given to William, son of Robert.

Wetherby

To enter Wetherby from the Leeds side of town, one has to cross the River Wharfe using a bridge which is a Scheduled Ancient Monument and a Grade II listed structure.

This route was once part of the Great North road which ran from London to Edinburgh straight through the middle of Wetherby; as can be imagined, Wetherby was a notorious bottleneck before the bypass was built which avoids the lovely bridge and the town centre.

Templar mill at Wetherby Bridge. (Courtesy of the Wetherby Historical Trust Archive)

Etching showing the Templar's mill and the weir at Wetherby Bridge. (Courtesy of the Wetherby Historical Trust Archive)

Pausing to look upriver, there are some fine new buildings on the right where once some Templar property stood. In the thirteenth century, there were two mills there which disappeared in time, though the ruins were still visible as late as 1930. There was also a chapel on the same bank but on the opposite side of the bridge dedicated to St Mary. The artist Thomas Girtin painted the scene around 1800 when the chapel was still standing and a print of his work hangs in a local supermarket.

Ribston's Templar chapel

Near the village of Little Ribston, a long drive leads from the road to a Knights' Templar chapel; about 50yds along the path is an ancient earth-built burial mound marked by a large upright stone. Glimpses of a grand house can be seen as the drive winds around to a bridge from around the eighteenth century, guarded at one end by two lodges. Over the bridge and past a weir, following the curve of the River Nidd, at last the chapel can be viewed peeping out from thick foliage.

All that remains of the Ribston Preceptory is the chapel, which now has the seventeenth-century Ribston Hall tacked on to one of its walls. Seven pairs of

Ribston chapel doorway.

Ribston chapel, showing the later house tacked onto the side.

Stained glass window in Ribston's Templar chapel showing St Andrew flanked by a Knight Templar and a Hospitaller. (Courtesy of Simon Brighton)

pews are ranged down the nave with each pew being big enough for about three people on one side and two on the other. What really catches one's attention are the stained glass windows illustrating the chapel's connection with the Templars, the Hospitallers and Ribston's benefactor, Sir Robert de Ros. The chapel was dedicated to St Andrew and one of the stained glass windows shows the saint standing with a Templar on one side of him and a Hospitaller on the other.

The chapel, in common with other Templar ecclesiastical buildings, has an alignment to herald the sunrise at 33 degrees to the north of east (rather than the perfect east-west line) on 22 July, which is the feast day of Mary Magdalene; a favourite saint of the Templars.

Outside the chapel, the ground gently slopes to the river for about 250yds. The chapel sits comfortably in a wide, generous bend in the river and is bounded by it on three sides. There are rolling, undulating meadows as far as the eye can see, cows munch contentedly all around, and there is peace and tranquillity; a truly pastoral scene. The devout Templars would surely have found this a splendid place

Interior of the chapel at Ribston. (Courtesy of Simon Brighton)

to have had their chapel, to meditate on the vows taken and to be sure they were carrying out God's work. About half a mile away there is a stand of trees which has a rookery; perhaps the remains of the original woodland gifted to the Templars.

An argument

In 1231, Ribston chapel was the basis for a row between the Templars and Matthew of Cantilupe, who was the local priest. There are some interesting references to other members of the clergy in different parts of the country who share his surname. One of them, Thomas Cantilupe, was even canonised and his tomb lies in Hereford Cathedral.

Our Ribston Cantilupe was on the receiving end of the Templars' wrath when he was alleged to have enclosed common pasture. He, in turn, said that they had not only enclosed a spring in Ribston churchyard, but had also built a chapel there. This group of Templars seems to have been a particularly diplomatic lot because the matter was sorted out to everyone's satisfaction. The Templars kept their chapel on condition that Matthew of Cantilupe's parishioners were denied access to it and did not bury their dead in its graveyard. They also released the spring from their enclosed land. In return, Matthew kept his 12 acres of enclosed pasture, so everyone was happy.

Art & architecture

During the Templar timeline of 1100–1312, art and architecture underwent vast changes. Traditionally, the onset of Gothic art is marked by Abbot Suger; during his abbacy of 1122–51 and when the rebuilding of the monastery of St Denis, near Paris took place. Decoration and other features of this building were to have far reaching effects upon architecture throughout Europe and would, by the sixteenth century, become known as the Gothic period, which was originally a derogatory term.

The high quality of work from about 1250 leaves us a body of work in various media which includes manuscripts, needlework, paintings, murals and stained glass which together demonstrate a complete artistic production. Small examples show the breadth and depth of work throughout this time.

The loop in the River Nidd which enfolded Ribston Preceptory.

By around 1250, art had emerged as having a distinctive style, though there is a lack of evidence to show what people actually thought about the emergent art of the Middle Ages. So unfortunately, we do not have any idea what reaction there was to the immense flowering of the various styles of architecture that gradually merged into the Gothic style. William of Sens was one of the great names of English architecture in the twelfth century, but unfortunately, there are no accounts of his training or his early life, nor do we know where he travelled and worked after his building of the great Canterbury Cathedral.

We do know that both Greek and Roman art was transported to and transposed into some of the cathedrals at this time. For instance, mosaic was used in St Denis by Abbot Suger and Roman antique statues found their way to Winchester thanks to Henry of Blois in 1151. The Abbot of Westminster returned from Rome in 1269 with men and materials to build a marble pavement in his new church at Westminster.

This was certainly an era for the prolific building of cathedrals: Laon was begun in 1165; Canterbury in 1179; Wells in 1180; Chartres in 1194; Rheims in 1210; Salisbury in 1220; and Burgos in 1222, to name but a few. England did not, of course, follow any style slavishly as can be seen by the magnificent York Minster, which was determined to be different. First, York is uncommonly wide. Its massive width makes it hard to draw a comparison with any other cathedral. It has a mixture in the design of the 'ribs' and the shafts that support the ribs run unbroken to the floor. There is no tribune gallery and the tracery of the clerestory windows forms a continuous pattern with the arcade of the triforium. York is magnificently different.

Quite often within a village, the church was the only stone building to be seen. There are a few Saxon churches remaining in England, but our older churches are predominately of Norman design which carried a distinctive style.

However, the Templars and Hospitallers developed a different design – that of the round church. While the round church was a hallmark of the Knights Templar, it was not used exclusively by them, as some would claim. Little Maplestead in Essex is a round church which was founded by the Knights Hospitaller in 1184. The Holy Sepulchre in Cambridge, built around 1130, was originally a Wayfarers chapel. The Knights Templar had an immense amount of building knowledge obtained, it is assumed, from the interaction they had with the Saracens. Indeed, when the 'new' building at the Temple Church on Fleet Street began, the Order imported masons from the Holy Land. There was also a company of masons based at the preceptory in Metz in eastern France. One name which is known is that of Jean Clowange, the master mason of the Order of the Temple in Lorraine.

The Knights Templar's wisdom in the art of geometry in relation to buildings was demonstrated by their involvement in the building of many of the finest cathedrals. Templar masons used their knowledge of geometry in cathedrals such as Chartres and Amiens, among many others. These cathedrals drew many pilgrims; apart from the relics that the cathedrals are said to have, another reason they were visited was because they also claimed to have a resonance with the divine harmony created by God in the formulation of the world through Templar designs. The Templars are reputed to have used much of their enormous wealth to help build these great cathedrals, as well as to support the armies in the Middle East. This is one explanation as to the sudden flowering of cathedrals across Europe.

Many of the mural paintings have been lost due to the nature of the art. However, small pockets do survive; we have all seen scraps of it here and there in churches and cathedrals. However, some still survive in secular buildings such as Windsor Castle.

On the whole though, it is religious art that survives rather than secular art, as during battles, castles were destroyed while churches were saved. Their art was well respected and looked upon as an extension of God's work. The famous Bayeux Tapestry has survived primarily because it was housed in a church.

The murals in the upper church of Francis of Assisi, decorated in about 1280, survives very well, as does the Capella dell'Arena in Padua. There, the walls are completely covered in frescos by Giotto, thought to be painted in 1303. Giotto is generally thought to be associated with the Renaissance era; however, he does come into our timeline. Giotto cracked the art of translating lifelike figures into paintings and sculptures. For this, he owed a great debt to the Byzantine artists, for they had achieved the finesse of painting soft drapery which seemingly enfolded the figure. They also achieved the shading of light and dark areas of faces, all of which totalled up to beautiful lifelike images. Giotto rediscovered the art of creating depth on a flat surface from the Byzantines.

In Westminster Abbey, there is a panel painting of St Peter which demonstrates a distinctive delicacy of painting. The elongated figure gives off an aura of carrying a weighty responsibility; he holds his symbol of a golden key in graceful fingers. The soft flowing drapery indicates a vital achievement in figure painting of the time.

The other flowering during the Gothic period is the art of the beautiful and often divinely delicate stained glass which can be seen in almost all of the Gothic cathedrals and is simply stunning to look at.

The exquisite and sometimes astonishing manuscripts are in a class of their own. In England, it was a golden time for this art form. Alphonso, the third son of King Edward I, had a Psalter made for him just prior to his death. The delicacy of the figure painting is a delight and together with the vibrancy of the border decoration, takes this Psalter beyond other contemporary work; in particular, other Parisian works. Another Psalter that stands above others is associated with the abbey of Peterborough. A luxuriously extravagant work, it encapsulates the visible world in a variety ways. It is full of vitality with an extraordinary observation of people, creatures and flora.

Matthew Paris, an Englishman, produced a manuscript of *The Life and Times of St Alban* painted about 1260. It shows the king with his architect visiting a building site and workers can be seen carrying out their tasks. Paris was also a chronicler of his time and wrote the *Historia Maior* in 1223. One of the paintings in it shows Christ on horseback accompanied by crusaders. This accentuates the fact that they were the soldiers of Christ.

Many of the Psalters are associated with East Anglia which seems gives rise to the notion of an East Anglian school of painting. What is for sure is that the English Psalters are a truly magnificent body of work.

The timeline of the Middle Ages has perpetuated a myth that it lacked any kind of movement in regard to art. If nothing else, hopefully this myth has, in part, been dispelled.

Wetherby market

Wetherby's flourishing market was mentioned earlier in this chapter. It is held on Thursdays, just as it has been since 1240 when, on 15 November, King Henry III granted a charter to the Templars, giving them the right to hold one. The market wasn't held in Wetherby originally, but about three miles further north in Walshford. In 1227, the Master of the Temple had paid £10 for the privilege, together with the right to hold an annual fair. The Templars didn't get as much business in Walshford as they would have liked, so they used their influence and got both the market and the fair moved to Wetherby. This did not please Margery de Rivers, who owned the manor of Harewood, who felt the market to be damaging to her manor and made her feelings known. However, everything was sorted out and on 18 November 1242, the matter was amicably settled to everyone's satisfaction. The fair was held over a three-day period consisting of the vigil day, the feast day and the following day celebrating the Feast of James the Apostle on 25 July. Although the market continues, the fair does not. Maybe there remains a very loose connection to it though, as the local Anglican church, built in 1839, is called St James.

With the exception of the Knights Templar, their tenants and the clergy, there was something that everyone visiting Wetherby market would have had in common with each other and with the nobility. They had to pay tithes and taxes.

Tithes & taxes

English churches were first granted the right to receive tithes by King Ethelwulf as far back as AD 855. However, it wasn't until the Statute of Westminster in 1285 that tithes had real legal standing. It was the nineteenth century before that law was repealed by Sir Robert Peel's government.

Tithes were a tax on all farm produce for the year; it was not a tax on money. One tenth of everyone's harvest had to be paid to the Church, no matter how meagre the harvest might be. Churches often had enormous barns in which to store the grain they were given. The one tenth didn't stop with crops, but included animals and products. The tenth colt or calf to be born had to be handed over to the Church. If people only had one or two animals, then instead, they had to pay an obole for each one, which was a coin that weighed the same as ten or twelve grains of the locally grown crop. If they made cheese, either the tenth one had to be handed over or the milk produced on the tenth day. Even bees had to pay up, a tenth part of their honey being handed over.

Taxes were another matter altogether and were based on land value. Initially started in the late tenth century and called geld, this tax later became known as carucage. Almost a hundred years after the Domesday survey of William the

Wetherby market charter and seal. (Courtesy of Yorkshire Archaeological Society)

Conqueror, another review was ordered by Henry II in 1166. Landowners had to submit details of their holdings, tenants and the service they owed. Henry was always short of money and it is thought that this time he was motivated by the need to raise some cash to pay for his son to be knighted and for his eldest daughter's wedding. He later took steps to standardise the country's coinage, but with his eye on being able to maximise taxation in future.

Taxation was an irregular affair at this time with finance, or aids, being raised as and when needed. For example, Henry II also introduced the Saladin tithe to help pay for the Third Crusade. Strictly speaking, it was an ecclesiastical tithe, but it needed Henry's agreement and cooperation to make it work. This tax meant that everyone had to give one tenth of rents and movable goods. The money had to be collected in the presence of the local parish priest, and either one Templar or one Hospitaller and various royal and ecclesiastical nominees. The only people exempt from paying the Saladin tithe were the clergy and knights who had taken the Cross. Henry fell into this last group as he had promised to go on crusade as part of his penance for the murder of Thomas Becket – but in the end, he never got to the Holy Land.

Henry wasn't the only king to raise money through taxing the English population. Edward I antagonised his barons by his imposition of unjust taxes to pay for his campaigns in Wales. Richard the Lionheart raised taxes to pay for the Third Crusade almost as soon as he became king. The English were hit with further taxes to pay his ransom of 150,000 marks to the Holy Roman Emperor Henry VI after Richard's capture. His successor, John, increased taxes to pay for his defeat by rebels in Brittany. He also exploited his barons by demanding and getting thousands of marks from them – an unprecedented action. It's little wonder that they rebelled against him!

A further tax that is worth a mention is scutage. It was another of Henry II's money-raising ideas which he put into place in 1159. Every knight was given the option of getting out of military service by making a cash payment in lieu, the money being used to maintain paid armies. A knight's other option was to pay someone to go in their place.

Fruit

Another legacy of Ribston is in the form of an apple – although it wasn't around when the Templars were there. The Ribston Pippin was raised there in the early eighteenth century from a pip brought over from Rouen. It is described as being sweet, crisp and more acid than the Cox apple. These days it is described as a 'heritage apple', whose trees are still obtainable if you fancy planting one in the garden. It is alleged to have the highest vitamin C content of any apple.

The Normans introduced fruits to this country which were not native. On the whole, they were various kinds of apples which were either brought with them or which they bred here, such as Haute Bonte from France and the English Pearmain and Costards. They also brought cider apples with them. Edward I's Spanish wife, Eleanor of Castile, introduced the Blandurel apple to England.

Surprisingly, peaches were also introduced by the Normans and would have been known to the upper classes during Templar times. It's said King John died because he ate so many peaches and washed them down with ale. However, as he was suffering from dysentery at the time, that seems a more likely cause.

Our medieval people would also have been familiar with quinces and medlars, which had been introduced centuries before by the Romans. But such delights as pears, plums and cherries only arrived after the Templars had been disbanded. Most people would have collected and eaten wild fruits, but on the whole, raw fruit was viewed with suspicion and so was usually eaten cooked.

10

WHITLEY

(near Knottingly, c. 1248)

Whitley is a place of mystery and uncertainty. The site of the preceptory is unknown; experts disagree whether there actually was a preceptory there at all and it is by no means certain that if indeed there was one, whether the Whitley which lies to the south of Temple Hirst is the right Whitley!

The village lines the busy A19 just south of where it crosses the M62. The majority of the houses are comparatively modern, with just the odd slightly older property here and there. One of the latter properties is called Manor Farm and is of interest only because some authorities maintain that the Templars had a manor there, not a preceptory. There are certainly medieval fishponds in the vicinity which, although now choked with weeds, could have belonged to either a manor or a preceptory.

The preceptory

Whitley earns its place as a preceptory in this book for one major reason – a man called Robert de Layton (or Langton) was described as its preceptor. It is thought that a manor or grange here may originally have formed part of the Temple Hirst estates and only became a preceptory in its own right much later on. Quite when its status was raised to that of a preceptory is unknown, although the beginning of the fourteenth century has been suggested. The manor of Whitley was certainly owned by the Templars prior to 1248 and in that year they were given a grant of free warren there. Free warren meant they had the king's permission to kill certain species of game within a specified area.

The English Knights Templar were no strangers to dispute on their home ground and Whitley was at the centre of one of them. There was a chapel there which was affiliated to the lovely thirteenth-century church of St Edmunds at Kellington. Robert de Piron, Temple Hirst's preceptor, maintained that the chapel's tithes belonged to his order, while the Abbot of Selby felt strongly that they belonged to his abbey. History doesn't record who won.

Just on the edge of Whitley village is a tiny place called Whitley Thorpe. Turning off the A19, and travelling along a series of narrow lanes criss-crossing the flat expanse of fields, ahead is the only rising ground in the area. In one of the grassy fields at the top of the hill there are the unmistakable signs of a long since dried up

St Edmund's Church, mother church to the Templar chapel in Whitley.

moat. It encompasses a square of slightly raised ground and the whole field is full of the hummocks that are often suggestive of former structures hidden beneath them. It is described as a 'moated Templar grange' site and is a Scheduled Monument. Given its location atop the highest point in the area and its defensive moat feature, one can't help wondering if this was, in fact, the place where Robert de Layton carried out his duties as a preceptor.

Magna Carta

Whatever the truth of the matter, thirty-three years before the Templars were granted their free warren, one of the most significant events in English history occurred: the creation of Magna Carta.

Think of Magna Carta and one thinks of King John. But the Knights Templar were also very much involved in this immensely important occasion, one way or another, an event that formed basis for the law of habeas corpus in England, the

Declaration of Independence in the USA and the Universal Declaration of Human Rights by the United Nations.

Originally the charter's intention was to safeguard the interests of English 'free men'. This excluded the majority of the population since they weren't 'free men' but were owned by the lords on whose land they lived and worked. Four of the clauses are still valid today, almost 800 years after they were first written; and since we are all now 'free', they apply just as much to us as they did to the 'free men' all those centuries ago. Clause 39 states that nobody can be 'seized or imprisoned, or stripped of his rights or possessions, or outlawed or exiled, or deprived of his standing in any other way . . . except by the lawful judgement of his equals or by the law of the land'. The next clause is short but powerful and to the point. It says: 'To no one will we sell, to no one deny or delay right or justice.' The very first clause deals with the freedom of the English Church and Clause 13 gives the city of London the freedom to have the benefit of 'all its ancient liberties and free customs, both by land and by water'. It goes on to allow that all other cities, boroughs, towns and ports can do the same.

To understand how Magna Carta came about in the first place and how the Templars fitted into its creation, it is necessary to backtrack to 1199 when King John came to the throne. The first thing the Templars did was to pay John £1,000 and a fine palfrey in return for his confirmation of their rights and privileges. Over time, he gave them land in various parts of England and a good relationship was built up which was later to stand John in good stead.

A few years into his reign, the king quarrelled with Pope Innocent III over who should be Archbishop of Canterbury. He was determined that the post holder should be his own choice of candidate and refused point blank to allow the Pope's man, the Englishman Stephen Langton, to even enter the country. On top of that, he expelled the monks from Canterbury. As a result of all this, in 1206, the Pope placed an interdict on England and Ireland which meant that everyone was barred from receiving the sacrament, or indeed from taking part in any form of religious ceremony. The exceptions were baptism and the confession of the dying. John simply saw this as an opportunity to confiscate all of the Church's property and was therefore excommunicated in 1209.

The Knights Templar became involved in travelling between England and Rome, trying to broker a diplomatic solution to all of this. Eventually the Pope sent his legate to Dover to negotiate further and it is said that he sat in one room and the king in another. Two Templars went back and forth between the pair of them, helping to thrash out an agreement. It ended on 15 May 1213 with King John handing over his English and Irish kingdoms to the Pope, together with nine gold marks to receive absolution. He also had to agree to pay homage to the Pope. John wasn't actually too concerned about losing England and Ireland, since he valued his French possessions much more highly.

The Church may have been annoyed with John, but so were his barons for different reasons. A hundred years before John came to the throne, Henry I had granted a 'Charter of Liberties', sometimes called the 'Coronation Charter'. This bound the king to the law and addressed certain abuses of royal power that affected the barons. It was largely ignored until 1215 when Magna Carta was drawn up, which was very closely based on that earlier charter.

Early in 1215 the barons tried but failed to get Magna Carta considered by King John and ended up fighting him in what is known as the Barons' Revolt. In May they managed to take and hold London because Londoners welcomed them with open arms. They promptly handed the city over to the French, who had landed in Kent on 21 May and held London and the Home Counties with an army of 35,000 men. It was to be some months after John's death in 1216 before the French finally left in 1217.

During the Barons' Revolt, John had managed to hold on to the rest of the country. There must have been some sort of successful negotiation because on 10 June 1215, the king, the barons and the major churchmen all met up at Runnymede. It is said that John had spent the previous night at the Temple in London and was accompanied to Runneymede by his good and very influential friend, the Knight Templar Aymeric St Mawr, Master of the Temple in England. If that is true, then either the French didn't hold the whole of London or Aymeric had enough influence to allow John free passage.

Magna Carta itself reads more like a list of grievances than a document destined to underwrite such important modern freedoms as it has done. Clauses deal, among other things, with inheritance issues, marriage of widows and daughters of dead barons, guardianship of land for under age heirs, debts owed to anyone, especially Jews, misuse of power by royal officials and general misuse of power by the king. Clauses 58 and 59 are a bit different in that they demand the freeing of royal Welsh and Scottish hostages held by John.

During the meeting at Runneymede, it is thought that there wasn't a completed document to be signed, but that notes were drawn up upon which the final document would be based. John simply signed the notes. The first draft was not called Magna Carta, but 'Articles of the Barons' and the final version did not emerge until very much later. It was reissued in 1216 by the nine-year-old Henry III, or more likely his regent, William Marshall. A third version was issued in 1225 and the document was finally ratified in 1295 by Edward I but with many of the original clauses removed.

Many copies of Magna Carta would have been made because by law all charters had to be read out to the whole population. Since they were all in Latin, it is doubtful if people of the peasant classes would have understood what these charters were all about. Now only seventeen copies of Magna Carta remain. Two are kept at the British Library, one at Salisbury Cathedral and one at Lincoln Cathedral. The Bodleian Library in Oxford holds a further four copies, three of which date from 1217 and one from 1225. Another copy was in private hands in America until December 2007, when it was auctioned and an American lawyer paid over £10 million pounds for it. The remaining copies are in libraries and archives in Australia and America.

Local travel

As mentioned earlier, the A19 runs through Whitley now, but back in the twelfth century, travel in the area wasn't so easy. The district consisted of low-lying fenlands and was often flooded, so a ridge or causeway was built, with deep ditches on either side. Its route appeared to link Knottingley, Whitley and Eggborough.

People travelled much more in the Templar period than one might suppose. The Order's preceptors travelled between the different preceptories and attended an annual conference at the Temple in London. Pilgrims, knights and soldiers were obvious travellers whose journeys could have taken them long distances and to foreign countries, but there would have been many local people making journeys within and outside Yorkshire. They would have been taking their wares to different markets, which were not allowed to be held on the same day or too close to each other. Customers weren't always from the local town or vill, but had to travel in from the surrounding countryside. There were itinerant tradesmen and women who plied their trade wherever they could find work.

There were no 'main' roads as we know them, but there were certainly well-worn traditional tracks all over the country. The use of some of them was restricted to carts, carriages and packhorses because of the problem of being delayed by pedestrians blocking the way forward. The Luttrell Psalter shows a stylish, upmarket four-wheeled carriage pulled by five horses. The occupants are obviously important people, probably rich landowners. The same book also has an illustration of a much simpler two-wheeled hay cart. As has been mentioned in chapter 7, river traffic was commonplace to move goods from place to place, as were the coastal routes between English ports. So although some people never left the immediate vicinity of their birthplace, many others were certainly on the move.

11

COPMANTHORPE

(near York, c. 1258)

To the east of the A64 heading towards the great city of York lies the bustling village of Copmanthorpe. The central area of the village has been designated a conservation area which takes in the lovely twelfth-century church of St Giles, Main Street and Low Green. 'Copmanthorp' points to Danish origins and the name remains the same in the Domesday Book; just when the 'e' at the end of the name was added is open to speculation.

The preceptory

The Knights Templar had a preceptory at Copmanthorpe certainly by 1258. The actual date of the grant is indeterminate but the manor is mentioned as belonging to the Order in a charter by William de Ros who died earlier that year. William Malbys gave the Order Copmanthorpe and other lands and property on certain conditions. These were that they must support a chaplain to celebrate and pray in the chapel for himself and the souls of his departed relatives.

Aerial photographs show a cropmark system of fields to the west of the Knights Templar preceptory; these consist of three long enjoined enclosures. The photographs also show a medieval windmill mound and boundary ditches and the possible site of fish ponds.

The Order's holdings

A return in 1292 shows that the preceptor of Copmanthorpe was the keeper of the mills below the castle at York. These mills were given to the Templars by Roger de Mowbray in 1185. At the time they were rented out for 15½ marks. At the same time, the Templars held other lands in York. These comprised 3 tofts, which the Templars had bought, plus another which had been gifted to them by Thomas Usam, an important resident in York. Added to this, Henry III gave them a further piece of land adjoining the mills. The king also granted the Templars timber for the repair of the mills in 1231.

By the time of the suppression of the Order in 1308, their lands had swelled with a messuage (a dwelling house with out-buildings and land) with a garden, three plots of land and rent from a chapel.

Field where Copmanthorpe Preceptory once stood, showing the flatness of the landscape.

Castle Mills

The only name known who had been a preceptor at Copmanthorpe was Robert de Rey, who, together with the chaplain of the Castle Mills chapel, was accused in 1292 of setting nets below the mills to catch the king's fish. However, Robert de Rey was still the preceptor the following year!

Castle Mills were really vital to the city although their exact location cannot be agreed upon. However, we do know that around 1215 the mills did not use a dam that had been constructed on the River Foss, but used a ditch built at this time with water running from the Foss, although this is not thought to have been of any great distance. It appears that the mills were situated on the west bank of the river, judging by a description of a piece of land granted to the Templars in 1231. It seems that the ditch did not work the mills for very long as they were moved to the dam site on the River Foss.

There are records that show during the fourteenth and fifteenth centuries, the mills needed quite a lot of upkeep to maintain them in good order. After the suppression of the Templars, the mills apparently fell into total disrepair. As early as 1316, the mills needed to be virtually rebuilt and again in 1348, further work was required. The Crown finally came into possession of the mills sometime after 1450. First the mills had passed to Knights Hospitallers, then, John de Mowbray, who had mounted a claim against the Hospitallers, owned them; later the mills had several owners. It was then found by the Crown that successive keepers of the mills had not only allowed them to fall in to disrepair but that they had not properly maintained them at all.

Jewellery, fine goods & trade

York was the most important city in the north and as such, there were many trades carried on there. Apart from the usual collection of trades associated with the larger cities and towns, York, together with cities such as London and Lincoln, demonstrated the increase of wealth through the variety of their shops. That wealth was predominately created by the wool trade and was shown by the increase of luxury goods available. Quite often shops were also the workroom where prospective buyers could peruse the goods. However, in the case of two luxury items in particular, this was not always the case. Jewellery and luxury material shops were a measure of wealth in a city and often these were on a footing that we could recognise today.

The Sumptuary laws of the thirteenth century came into force in England which, in short, prevented townsfolk from wearing girdles and coronals which were made of pearls and gemstones. Since these laws debarred the artisans from wearing gems, gold and silver, it demonstrates how the status of jewellery had become widespread – well beyond the limits of the nobility. At this time, the Sumptuary law was probably used to maintain class distinction.

Tokens of love have been in existence forever and jewels have always played their part in this demonstration of devotion. Italian merchants had always been in the forefront of supplying precious jewels from the East. Good glass imitations were often used for children and for funerary robes. However, fake jewellery was now in existence for the townspeople. Recipes for false pearls made from glass, albumen and snail slime were available and were sold in the shops, together with other glass 'gems' from Venice and Murano.

Lavish materials available for clothes were also more widespread, with merchants importing much more from the East and other parts of Europe. Yet another measure of affluence was due to the crusaders who returned to all parts of Europe with Turkish carpets. Although they were principally used on tables or hung on walls, such carpets were another luxury item of the thirteenth century.

Generally though, for the shopkeepers in the towns, it was hard graft. Their day began with the ringing of the Angelus bell at four or five o'clock, which announced the first Mass of the day; it also ended the night watchman's duties. Most of the shops opened at about 6 o'clock in order to give plenty of time for shopping in readiness for the first meal of the day taken between 9 and 10 o'clock. Many shops closed around 3 o'clock, while others remained open until dusk; these included the blacksmiths and, oddly enough, the barbers. However, when the curfew bell rang, everywhere closed down.

It was then that visiting merchants needed to ensure that they were either bedded down at an inn or outside the city limits. Foreign merchants had a hard time as they were forcefully regulated. They would have had to give local marketers a head start in selling their wares, as visiting merchants would have had to wait at least two hours before they could enter the market-place and begin selling their goods. Quite often the only way they could advertise themselves was to walk about shouting out what they had to offer.

Town criers

Another member of the community who had plenty to shout about was the Town Crier; these men were the main source of news for city dwellers. It wasn't until the time of William the Conqueror that a formal system of Town Criers was established in England. The appointment the Town Crier, or the 'bellman' as he was also known, was made by the civil authority, frequently the mayor, as it was a very important position. The job was often handed down from father to son as the position required absolute trust from every quarter and gave a certain standing in the community. His job was to keep the people informed on all kinds of issues. These could be matters of national importance like war, local happenings such as minor transgressions or important royal events. Anything and everything came by way of the Town Crier. The saying 'don't shoot the messenger' comes from this time as often the Town Crier would be bringing news of tax increases or other unwelcome news. In fact, it was a treasonable offence to harm a Town Crier since it was seen as an extension of harming the monarch, as he stood in the king's stead. Indeed, to this day, under old English law, it is still an offence to hinder or heckle or otherwise interfere with a Town Crier in the pursuance of his duty. The man in this privileged position was empowered to uphold the law and was seen as a staunch Royalist. He was also required to perform another duty. Walking about, ringing his bell, he would petition for prayers for the recently dear departed of people who had previously paid for the service. The shouting of 'Oyez, oyez' is derived from the old French meaning 'listen' or 'hear ye'.

Today there about 200 Town Criers in Britain, with thousands more throughout the English speaking world, so the job is alive and well. They do not have a guild as such, but do have a recognised fellowship.

Guilds

The earliest known guilds occurred in India about 3800 BC. However, guilds began to properly grow in Europe between the tenth and eleventh centuries. Prior to this, there had been religious fraternities and collectives for a long time. In tenth-century Europe, many changes were taking place and the growth of the various guilds was just one of them. There was a steady move to the townships and cities from the country which gave rise to the creation and formalisation of the various guilds. There were two types of guilds, the merchants and the craftsmen.

Merchants began to band together for their joint benefit and protection and gradually they began to lay down rules and regulations. These included a given standard of work, expected behaviour and a certain social status. By the thirteenth century, these guilds were recognised by most of Western Europe, although some towns and cities opted to remain 'free'. Over time, the merchant guilds welded an immense amount of power and became highly controlling, reaching their zenith of power by the fourteenth century. The merchants could be wholesale, retail, local or long distance in their trading. The guilds eventually organised the distribution and sale of all kinds of commodities, including staple foods and cloth. In time, this led to a very unhealthy state of affairs in many towns and cities.

The medieval guilds obtained high status and privileges; they wore ceremonial dress and had their own standards and banners, while their power, at times, cannot be underestimated.

As the power of the guilds gradually fell away and a decline set in, competition among individuals took its place. Today, the Chamber of Commerce is the nearest comparison we have to an overarching organisation similar to that of the merchant's guilds.

In Yorkshire, York was renowned for its Merchant Aventurers' Hall; it remains one of the finest surviving medieval guildhalls in the country. Though built a little later than the Templar timeline, previously York did have a strong fraternity and guild in honour of Jesus and the Virgin Mary. The York Merchants' guild was to eventually out-price itself in terms of cost in the export of goods. This eventually led to a cottage industry springing up throughout the Yorkshire Dales of weaving and the production of textiles and the total bypassing of York as an export centre. This industry grew and grew and ultimately led directly to the Aire and Calder canal being constructed for the movement of goods. By this time, the rivers into York were too silted up for large ship navigation. The York Company still exists and operates as a charitable organisation.

Craftsmen were the other type of guild and some of these kinds of guilds still exist to this day. Craftsmen were organised quite differently in some ways, but they did also maintain a standard of work and a code of behaviour, and within the social circle, a status when reaching the final accolade of master craftsman.

The guilds came about for mutual protection, but they would also limit the number of members to what a city or town could support as it would not do to strain the economics of a trade.

The guilds were made up of individual crafts such as bakers, silversmiths and leather-workers, to name just a few of the myriad different trades. Each craft set its own standard of work. A lad first became an apprentice, which lasted five to nine years. Following this, he became a journeyman; this allowed the chap to work with different masters of his craft. He needed to prove his technical skills and the mastery of his craft but by far the biggest hurdle was overcoming the 'inner circle' to become a master. A master craftsman had already proved his worth and he had status within their community. Generally, they were reluctant to admit others as a master, particularly if it was felt that there was enough of a trade already in the town, as it would cause financial constraints. It was the 'inner circle' who made the decision to admit another. The knowledge and status was jealously guarded by the Master. The importance of these guilds cannot be emphasised enough.

In Rosslyn Chapel near Edinburgh, there is an Apprentice Pillar. The story goes that a master craftsman went abroad to seek the wisdom to carve a pillar as requested by his patron. In his absence, his apprentice carved the pillar. When the master craftsman returned to find the pillar already exquisitely carved, he inquired as to who had carried out the work. On being told it was his own apprentice, he was so angry and so full of jealousy and resentment that he killed his apprentice with his mallet. There is a moral in there somewhere!

In most towns, unlike the merchants, the craftsmen grouped themselves together. Hence, we still see street names pertaining to certain trades; for example, Butchers Row or Brewers Lane.

Guilds carried out other duties in society. For instance, they may have provided for the dowries of the poor girls, provided funeral expenses and given aid to families of a departed craftsman. Also some public duties were expected such as policing the streets. In fact in York, it is still (apparently) legal to shoot a Scotsman with a bow and arrow if found within the city walls after dark!

One of the oldest of the craftsmen and perhaps the most well known is that of the stonemasons' guild. Their signatures can still be seen in cathedrals and churches across Europe, sometimes as many as three different marks on one huge column. The extravagance of the cathedrals that blossomed across Europe is without equal in epoch of time. The anonymous craftsmen who worked on them had immense vision. The Mason builder was a very highly-skilled designer and engineer and was, above all, an architect of renown. The massive structures, the airiness and with the interior often looking rather delicate and extremely graceful, it is no wonder medieval society was overawed and that they became places of mystical phenomenon.

There is one guild that cannot go unmentioned; it is that of the cordwainer, founded in Oxford in 1131. A cordwainer is a shoemaker, but not your average shoemaker; a cordwainer worked only with new leather of the finest quality for making shoes, whereas the cobbler mended old shoes. The name is an Anglicisation of the French *cordonnier*, which in turn was taken from the Spanish word *cordouan*. This word is a corruption of the Spanish town of Cordoba which was renowned for two crafts in particular. One was its silversmiths and the other was the production of a super soft leather. The Moors had a secret way of producing the soft and yielding leather. It was apparently made from the skin of the Musoli goat; then only found in a few places, among them Sardinia and Corsica. The crusaders brought back this secret from the Moors and the very best boots and shoes were made by the guild of cordwainers.

Miracle & mystery plays

Many of the guilds were very active producing the 'Miracle' plays. These plays were performed in the public arena and were normally of a sacred subject usually taken from the Bible; whereas 'Mystery' plays were normally about saints. The various guilds had favourite plays. The guild of goldsmiths often performed the 'Adoration of the Magi', while the shipwrights chose the story of Noah's Ark.

In York and Wakefield, these plays became very well known and whole communities came to watch them. Not all of the plays were of a sacred nature though; some had a jocular theme and some even erred on side of the satirical in format. York still performs plays each year which take place in an outside arena.

Women's position in society

Women did not have too much to shout about in the time of the Templars, though there are a few who protested against the male dominated world. The position of women was a confusing one; on the one hand Mary, mother of Jesus, was revered; on the other hand, women were vilified by the same Church as temptresses in league with the devil.

In the twelfth century, an idealistic view of women was provided by all the various aspects of the Church; monks, clergy and the rest, and whatever the articulated belief with regard to women was, it was given by the churchmen. This group of men were forbidden to marry and were therefore deemed to be celibate. So, in the twelfth century, the cult of the Virgin Mary was born and promulgated by the Church.

At the same time, malevolent, hell-fire and damnation sermons were being spewed out from the pulpit that put the ills of the entire world firmly at the feet of women. The noble classes were also very influential in promoting the ideas of their chaplains and bishops and yet, these two groups put together formed a minority in the population as a whole. The mass of people had no say in how the perception of women should be viewed.

While these two divergent images of women were being put forward, another concept was being engendered into the consciousness of the masses – that of chivalry. It was at this time that the idea of knights and fair maidens took hold. The idea that men should be chivalrous towards women persisted well into the twentieth century and in some quarters, even to this day!

Whether high or low born, a woman was a chattel bound to the land. An heiress or a manorial villein, land was the key that opened their future, for better or for worse. Marriages were almost always an arranged affair, organised and overseen either by parents or overlords. The most important consideration was one of finances and/or land. For the heiress, it was fortune and land holdings, for the manorial villein it was the extra work on the land that could be derived from a union and the subsequent offspring providing more workers.

The working classes, who outnumbered all the rest, remained uneducated and downtrodden. They toiled in the fields, worked in the home, carded, weaved and spun wool. They made cheese and butter, salted fish and dried the meat. On top of that, a woman may well have helped her husband or father in his work. The Luttrell Psalter shows women labouring in the fields and another picture shows them shearing sheep. On Sundays she would have stood in church and listened to sermons telling her she was the devil's spawn, while the Virgin Mary was idolised.

Ladies also had a mountain to climb as far as work was concerned, though not as hard or as high as her illiterate country sisters. A lady was important in her home, commanding quite a lot of power well beyond it. She had to run a huge house like a well-oiled machine. She had a mass of servants to organise, both inside and out, and had to be aware of what was happening among the villagers. She was akin to a good manager of a company of today, but without the income and perks. She was expected to take on the duties of pastoral care for young knights, to see that they had manners fit for the table and to tend to their spiritual needs in lieu of a priest. She also needed to be able to run her husband's estates during his absences, as well as to be proficient in a noble lady's pursuits in the home.

On the other hand, a lady who was *femme sole*, either a widow or unmarried, did have rights. In English common law, she could hold land and make a will, among other things. However, marriage saw an end to that; her lands became her husband's for the duration of their marriage and beyond, in certain cases. A woman with land was a woman of considerable significance; therefore, she could be abruptly given in marriage either as a maid or as a widow, whether she agreed or not. However, she could purchase the right to marry whom she wanted. Many lords and kings profited from this arrangement, so her lot was not too bad.

Perhaps the one class of women that began to crack this persistent dogma came from the lower middle classes. As trade boomed, more and more women became involved in all manner of occupations. The majority of women in trade were married, but by no means all. As the women became more and more entrenched in their trade work, so a very slow improvement in their status began to grow.

Strangely, bourgeois notions in literature were quite often hostile to these particular women, as it was deemed they were flying in the face of the 'courtly' code. Wives and daughters were used to helping husbands and fathers in their craft work. In the Middle Ages, there were many widows and unmarried daughters who carried on the craft after the death of the husband or father. Trades could range from pouch-makers, to dyers, to the complicated system of tracking and movement of merchandise dealing with ocean-going ships to small local craft carrying local produce and commodities. One woman was mentioned in the 1274 Rolls as a 'Merchant of the Staple', an established exporter of English wool to Calais.

Many unmarried women supported themselves as shop keepers such as drapers, pie shop or fishmongers; even being a wet nurse provided an income. Some married women carried on a business quite separate from their husbands, perhaps their late father's trade, for example.

Nunneries were also another avenue open women. Between the years of 1250 and 1540, there were about 130 nunneries, apart from the Gilbertines of which there were only ten. Most of the very famous houses were to be found in the southern part of England; however, they appear to have been most prolific in the north. They tended to be ranked as priories rather than abbeys due to the fact that they were often quite small with only a few nuns. They were often quite poorly endowed. As well as spiritual education, these places quite often provided other forms of education for the nuns; as well as the more formal education of writing and reading, they included medicinal knowledge of plants and herbs.

Nuns were drawn from a narrow circle, often from women of gentle birth. If there were a number of sons in the family a daughter was passed to the nuns, as this prevented the need of a dowry for marriage; the dowry to a nunnery was deemed much less and helpful in furthering the good deeds required for the afterlife.

Some women excelled and flowered in the spiritual life of a nun and examples can be found throughout the Middle Ages, not just in England but throughout Europe, such as Euphemia of Wherwell, Hildegard of Bingen, Catherine of Siena and Theresa of Avila.

12
THE END OF AN ERA

On 14 September 1307, King Philip IV of France sent secret orders to his officials across the country, in preparation for an event scheduled take place the following month. His instructions were explicit. On Friday 13 October, they were to arrest every Knight Templar in their area. This action was to have repercussions that stretched across the channel and reached up to touch the Order's Yorkshire contingent.

The French connection

There are several theories as to why King Philip took the action he did. They range from the refusal of the Templars to accept him into the Order as an honorary member, through to an honest conviction that the Templars were heretics, to a real need to get his hands on their wealth. Beyond France's borders, the belief was widely held that the key was money; the Italians were the leading bankers at the time and they were convinced of this. Whatever those motives were, Philip was ruthlessly determined to get rid of the Knights Templar wherever they existed, by whatever means necessary.

Seven hundred years later, modern historians continue to debate the king's motives. There are complex issues to be considered. Philip was a very pious man who believed, as his father and grandfather had done, that the French had replaced the Jews as God's chosen people. His role, as he saw it, was to honour his coronation vow to be their judge and protector. Given his belief in his exalted position, one has to wonder whether joining any religious order, even as an honorary member, might not be somewhat beneath him.

Philip is sometimes seen as a weak-willed monarch who surrounded himself with strong advisors. There is a school of thought which maintains that it was these advisors who saw the Templar wealth through covetous eyes and influenced Philip through a subtle whispering campaign. It is suggested that they used his great piety to advantage, saying that the Templars were heretics who wanted to usurp the king's authority and influence. They would, in this case, have reminded him of his vow to protect his subjects, knowing that the king took his coronation vows very seriously indeed.

There is also another dimension to this convoluted story and it does give some credence to the beliefs held by the Italian bankers. France was in a lot of financial trouble. Philip's grandfather, the saintly Louis IX, had taken part in the Seventh and Eighth Crusades, both of which were disastrous. Philip's father also left huge debts as a consequence of various military actions. French coinage was regularly debased, so there would eventually come a point when any taxes levied would be ineffectual. Therefore, due to high expenditure over an extended period, France's finances were in pretty poor shape. Templar wealth would solve that little problem.

To some extent, the Knights Templar could be said to have contributed to their own downfall. Over the years, they had made enemies both within and outside the Church. In Yorkshire, for example, the Cistercians frequently felt that land had been gifted to the Templars which they should have received. In the preceding chapters, various disagreements the Templars had were mentioned, but these are only a few examples of the many that took place – some of which ended up having to be settled in the local courts. Then there was the secrecy concerning initiation rites into the Order. This inevitably furnished their enemies with the opportunity to conjure up all sorts of charges, including the use of magic and witchcraft. The major charge against them was of heretical practices. On top of that, some people blamed the Order for the loss of the Holy Land, accusing them of cowardice and of fraternising with the enemy.

Acre had fallen to the Saracens in 1291, which led to the Christian armies departing the Holy Land which was really when the rot set in, heralding the beginning of the end. The major reason for the Knights Templar being established in the first place had been to protect pilgrims on their visits to the Middle East. They had developed into a fearsome, efficient fighting force that inspired both respect and hatred in their Saracen enemies. The only function left to them now was in the world of commerce – and the wealth they had accumulated in that arena produced enemies much closer to home.

The Templars were only answerable to the Pope, not to their countries' rulers or senior clergy. It would therefore be reasonable to assume that Pope Clement V would have taken steps to protect them. Indeed, on 27 October 1307 he wrote to Philip expressing his indignation at the arrests. And yet on 22 November, he issued a papal bull entitled 'Pastoralis Praeminentiæ', ordering the arrest of all Knights Templar everywhere and the confiscation of their property. His reason for finally succumbing to the king's wishes can be traced back to his predecessors, Pope Benedict XI and Pope Boniface VIII. Benedict had inherited a serious conflict between Philip and Boniface. Then he was taken ill suddenly and died, which some believe was attributable to the king ordering him to be poisoned. Whatever the veracity of this, it left the way open for Philip to install a French Pope whom he could influence and manipulate. This man was Clement V.

Clement initially condemned Philip's actions against the Knights Templar, annulled the trials and suspended the powers of both the bishops and their inquisitors. However, he was persuaded to issue his bull a month later. The king had simply threatened that if Clement did not do as he was told, then Philip would try Boniface posthumously for acts which would have destroyed the dead Pope's reputation. Rather than allow that to happen, Clement acquiesced to Philip's demands. He issued the bull ordering the Templars' arrest and trial. Within a month of the arrests, the first Parisian hearings and the first confession of the Grand Master of the Temple, Jacques de Molay, had all taken place.

There were 104 charges against the French Templars which included heresy, idolatry, sodomy and secrecy regarding their procedures, especially where initiation was concerned. Despite initially pleading their innocence, the Templars in France were tortured ferociously until they said what the king wanted to hear. Jacques de Molay later admitted that he had lied under torture in order to save his life. In the event, he only extended it for seven years as he was burned at the stake on 18 March 1314 after retracting his confession of guilt. He wasn't the first of the Brothers to suffer this fate as more than fifty French Knights Templar had been burned at the stake in 1310 for the same reason.

Not everyone believed the charges brought against the Order. A letter written in 1308 defended the Templars, referring to their torture and recognising that it would only stop if they lied. It alleges that they were unjustly oppressed, had been denied justice and a fair hearing and roundly condemned the action brought against them.

Action in England

In England, the allegations against the Templars were not viewed in the same way. For a start, not all of the charges levelled against the French Brothers were brought against their English counterparts. Nonetheless, there were still seventy-four alleged crimes to be answered for.

Philip had written to all heads of state whose countries were home to any Knights Templar, urging them to duplicate the action he had taken in France. This put Edward II in an awkward position as he was due to marry the French king's daughter, Isabella in 1308. Nonetheless, he responded with a refusal to act. He strongly protested Philip's actions, maintained that the Templars had committed no crimes in England and rejected the accusations against them. Furthermore, he wrote in a similar vein to the kings of Portugal, Castile, Aragon and Sicily. In those letters he accused Philip of greed and envy and encouraged them to ignore the French king's demands too.

Then Clement's papal bull arrived commanding the arrest of the Templars and the confiscation of their property. Edward had no choice but to obey its strictures. If he did not, he would be excommunicated which would have put his soul beyond the reach of Heaven. On top of that, his country would have been put under interdict with the same result for his people. He dared not disobey the Pope's instructions.

And so, just as Philip had done, at the end of December 1307, he sent secret orders for the arrests to be made. However, it was 9–10 January 1308 before this actually happened. The delay may have meant that the content of the secret orders became known and this enabled some members of the Order to escape to safety. If this was the case, it may explain why up to half a dozen of the Yorkshire preceptors were not among those arrested in the county. This, of course, is only conjecture, although they would almost certainly have been aware of what was happening in France. In the meantime, Edward felt he had carried out the spirit of the bull and that this would be the end of the matter, because in truth, he remained unconvinced that any of it was necessary. Unlike his future father-in-law, Edward wanted to do things legally, so he issued a royal writ to have a detailed inventory taken of everything the Templars owned. Until the arrival of the papal inquisitors, the Templars were more or less under open arrest. When the inquisitors insisted they were imprisoned, Edward made sure that their period of incarceration was made as comfortable as possible by not keeping them in close confinement. They were also allowed to take bedding and other possessions with them into prison and the king insisted that they were treated with respect. All of this applied to the Templars imprisoned in the Tower of London. In Yorkshire, they were treated even more casually, as will be seen later.

There were a total of 172 Templars arrested across England, Scotland and Ireland. Only fifteen of those were knights, the rest being made up of chaplains and sergeants. At their trials, all of them denied every major charge and only admitted to minor infringements, such as wearing cords under their clothes next to their skin.

Obviously, this was not what the inquisitors wanted to hear, so in December 1309 they requested the king's permission to use torture. Edward hesitated for months before finally agreeing to it in April the following year, and then only after the Pope had twice written to him ordering him to allow it. However, the king drew the line at the use of the rack or anything that would result in permanent mutilation or disabling of a limb. He stressed that under no circumstances was any blood to be spilt. He was uncomfortable with the idea of being associated with the Templars' torture, so he eased his conscience by instructing that they be moved from the Tower. They were to be taken to various prisons within London's city gates where they would become the responsibility of the sheriff. The latter was advised that he may allow the inquisitors to do whatever they wanted, providing it was within ecclesiastical law. By doing this, Edward felt himself removed from responsibility, which now fell to the City of London and the Church. His original instruction was sent in August, but it took a second letter before his instructions were finally carried out in October. In the event, it is uncertain whether any torture was actually carried out.

The Yorkshire Templars

Meanwhile, up in Yorkshire, things were somewhat different. Although the Templars were locked up in York Castle each night, they were free to stroll around the city during the day. They may even have taken a walk across town to look at the building work that was going on at York Minster where, in 1291, work had started on the western end of the nave. They certainly had considerable freedom and were obviously trusted to return to their quarters at night. This happy state of affairs did not go on indefinitely. In March 1310, the king sent orders that the prisoners were to be kept in safe custody and not allowed the liberty they had so far enjoyed.

Between four and six of the Yorkshire preceptors were arrested (depending on which source you read). These were Geoffrey des Arches from Temple Newsam, Ivo de Etton from Temple Hirst, William de la Fenne from Faxfleet and John de

Clifford's Tower, York Castle's keep atop a Norman motte, where the Templars were imprisoned.

Walpole from Temple Cowton and possibly William de Grafton, Preceptor of York (visiting Ribston at the time) and Robert de Hales from Foulbridge. Whether the remaining preceptors escaped or whether the positions had simply lapsed and not been filled, is open to speculation. At Westerdale for example, the preceptory's priest, Stephen de Radenage, was among those consigned to York Castle, but there is no mention of his superior. Numbers also vary regarding the other Templars who were imprisoned alongside the preceptors, ranging from fourteen to twenty-one. Although the majority of the prisoners were based in Yorkshire, there were also a few Templars from elsewhere.

On 12 August 1309, the Pope sent two bulls to William Greenfield, the archbishop of York who was in charge of the Templar detainees. One of the bulls condemned the Knights Templar, especially those in Yorkshire. The other authorized an official inquiry into their activities and nominated commissioners to carry out this inquiry. These were the Archbishop of York, the Bishops of Durham, Lincoln, Chichester and Orleans (which belonged to England at the time), together with the French abbots of Lagny and St Germain des Champs, the Pope's chaplain, M. Sicard de Vaur and Guy de Vichy, Rector of Hesh in the diocese of London. At first Greenfield ignored the Pope's orders as he found the whole issue so distasteful. He also told the Pope that the Bishops of Lincoln and Chichester could not act in Yorkshire. Considering that he had been consecrated Archbishop of York in France by Clement V only a short time before, one has to admire his courage in taking this stance. Something or someone made him change his mind because on 11 March 1310, by which time he was in London, he summoned a provincial council to be held in York on 20 May. Their remit was to investigate the allegations made against the Knights Templar held in that city. The provincial council, consisting of most of the northern senior clergy, adjourned their meeting when the Templars denied all charges against them.

These charges were based on hearsay and in modern England would not even have reached a court of law. Only one out of the fifty-six outside witnesses called said they had heard anything untoward about the Order. The other fifty-five had never heard of anything unseemly or improper relating to the Templars. In an effort to try and dig up dirt of some sort on them, in June, Greenfield sent a few of his clergy to question servants and retainers at the preceptories of Ribston with Wetherby, Temple Newsam, Temple Hirst, Faxfleet, Foulbridge, Westerdale, Penhill and Temple Cowton, as well as to some of their manors. As far as can be ascertained, these were wasted journeys since nothing new appeared to emerge.

Bearing in mind the hearsay nature of the charges, the sort of things that were alleged to have happened ranged from the heretical spitting on the cross, to homosexual orgies and lewd behaviour, to idolatry, particularly worship of a calf's head and dabbling in the occult. To give some idea of just how anecdotal the evidence was, one witness admitted that he had only heard about these aberrations *after* the Templars had been arrested!

The 'facts' that witnesses in York produced as evidence is fairly typical of the sort of thing said about them everywhere they were tried. For instance, John of Warrington (or de Nassington), an official of the Archbishop of York, said that he had been told by two knights that they once attended a banquet at Temple Hirst where a calf was worshipped. Another alleged that his wife had been lent a book by William de la Fenne and inside she found a loose piece of paper full of blasphemy against Christ. In his defence, the Faxfleet preceptor said that he remembered the book well even though he had given it to Lady Eure six years previously, but had no idea that it contained the note in question. One has to wonder why nothing had been said about it earlier!

On his deathbed, a Templar called Patrick de Rippon was alleged to have confessed to an Augustinian friar (who had since died), who told the Rector of Crofton (near Wakefield) about his admission to the Order. He allegedly said that he had been stripped to his shirt, taken to a secret chamber, made to spit on the crucifix and dishonour it 'in a more gross way' and finally to kiss and worship the image of a calf. Another friar maintained that following a meal at Ribston, the chaplain had told him that when he was at the chapel in Wetherby, he saw an orgy taking place. Time and again the evidence was based on statements like 'I know someone who knew someone...'

Despite his reluctance, on 21 February 1311, Archbishop Greenfield was forced to summon another provincial council. All the prelates and dignitaries of the north were invited to attend the meeting which took place on 24 May, and which turned out to be the first of many. The object was to try to decide what course of action should be taken. Some accounts say that the king then decided the Templars should be sent to London, since they were being treated far too well in York. Others suggest that the Yorkshire Templars spent the entire time in York. It is thought that they were tried there and that their reconciliation and absolution took place before the south door of the Minster, the south transept having been completed a few decades earlier.

In the end, no Templars in England were put to death and a compromise of sorts was reached. Most of the British Templars publicly renounced their heretical behaviour, except for the Master of England, William de la More, and a Templar called Himbert Blanke. More refused to ask for absolution when he was innocent of the charges against him. Both of them died in prison.

The rest of the Templars, however, did ask for forgiveness and reconciliation with the Church. They were given absolution and were required to carry out penances, after which they were each given pensions of 4 pennies a day. If they wished to continue to lead a monastic life they were given the option of joining existing monasteries, which many of them did. This didn't sit particularly well with the monasteries concerned, but generally they had to put up with it. Kirstall Abbey was landed with Richard de Shefeld, but he'd had enough after a year and disappeared. The Cistercians were delighted to see the back of him as they found him surly and rude. Rievaulx Abbey refused to host a Templar at all and a Brother who chose to live at Fountains Abbey was considered disruptive and insolent.

The Council of Vienne & the Pope

To make absolutely certain that he got rid of the Knights Templar once and for all, King Philip pressured Pope Clement V to convene the Fifteenth Ecumenical

Council. Its main purpose was to make 'provision in regard to the Order of Knights Templar, both the individual members and its lands. . .' There were other issues to be deliberated too, but destroying the Templars was the major consideration.

The meeting was held in Vienne, a little town not far from Lyon in Provence. Hence it has gone down in history as 'The Council of Vienne'. The archbishops of every church province with two or three bishops had to attend, and those bishops had to transfer their voting rights to their colleagues who attended. Naturally the Pope and his cardinals also formed part of the synod, as did some abbots. The actual number of participants is uncertain and, as is so often the case, the authorities can't agree but it was thought to be somewhere between 114 and 300.

Delays occurred, but finally the Council convened on 16 October 1311, when the first formal session was held in Vienne's cathedral. A commission was appointed to examine the official records concerning the Order. From this commission, a smaller committee of archbishops and bishops was formed. Most of them agreed that the Order should be given the right to defend itself as the evidence against them was so flimsy. This didn't suit King Philip at all, so he went to Vienne himself in March 1312 and in a letter to the Pope dated 2 March, he demanded that the Templars be suppressed. Clement V felt intimidated by Philip's nearby army and therefore had no option but to do as he was told, even though some of the Council did not agree to it. The Bull of Suppression was issued on 22 March 1312 and The Order of the Poor Knights of Christ of the Temple of Solomon in Jerusalem ceased to exist – sort of.

In writing the bull, the Pope applied a clever piece of canon law and used ambiguous terminology which enabled him to suspend, rather than suppress, the Order altogether. He neither condemned nor abolished it, and declared that the trials did not prove the charge of heresy. He gave the Templars a non-definitive sentence banning them from using either their name or their distinctive symbols on pain of excommunication. It didn't really make much difference to them in real terms. The Order was universally disbanded and Philip made sure that the Grand Master Jacques de Molay and others burned at the stake.

In 2002, an extra dimension was given to the whole affair. A document called the Chinon Parchment was found during the course of some research on an entirely different matter. It showed that the Pope had secretly sent three of his trusted emissaries to Chinon, where Jacques de Molay and other Templars were imprisoned. Their remit was to talk to the Grand Master and some of the preceptors '. . . in order that we might with diligence examine the truth. . . ' The investigation took place over a three day period from 17–20 August 1308. Satisfied with the answers they were given, the papal legates granted the Templars absolution in the presence of witnesses. The fact that the Pope was armed with this information may perhaps explain why he worded the Bull of Suppression so carefully.

Yorkshire Templar property

In England, Edward II was absolutely meticulous in dealing with the Templars' property. At the same time that the arrests took place, the sheriffs were instructed to take an inventory of movable property at each preceptory and manor and to arrange for an estimate of its value. Those entrusted to do the latter were perhaps not quite as honest as they might have been, but on the whole, a second inventory after the trials revealed that only food and minor items went missing. There was certainly no sign of the enormous treasure which popular legend persists in asserting existed.

At the time of the first inventory in 1308, Temple Newsam had a total value of £174 3s 3d and was considered to be one of the wealthiest preceptories in the country. The only item of any great value was a chalice worth 60s, but the chapel where it was kept was very plainly furnished. However, other Yorkshire preceptories were even wealthier. Faxfleet had a value of £290 4s 10d, with the contents of its chapel being worth a remarkable £12. Foulbridge Preceptory, together with its estates at Allerston and Wydale was valued at £254 3s 2d, while its chapel contained four crosses '. . . two with images and two without.'

Although Ribston and Wetherby formed one preceptory, for some reason, the sheriff valued them separately. Wetherby was worth £120 7s 8d; Ribston included holdings at North Deighton and Lound and were valued at £267 13s. Both St Andrew's and St Mary's chapels contained simple furnishings, but the Ribston chapel contained two silver cups, three masers (small shallow wooden bowls embellished with silver) and ten silver spoons – no other Yorkshire preceptory had as much secular plate.

Whitley was valued at £130 15s 10d and three saddle-horses were found there, two of which belonged to William de Grafton, Preceptor of Yorkshire, the other belonged to Whitley's preceptor, Robert de Langton. Just up the road, Temple Hirst was surprisingly only valued at £64 15s 2½d with Kellington Church contributing more than half to that sum.

The only things mentioned at Penhill were a chalice worth 20s, together with a few books and vestments. However, sheep and pigs were found on various of their holdings, as well as a few cows, horses, goats, oxen and doves. Westerdale's value came in at £32 19s 6d and Temple Cowton at about £100. The latter preceptory's chapel contained two hanging bells worth 26s and two handbells valued at 12d.

Finally, Copmanthorpe, which was valued at £80 16s 2d, with its mills in York being worth £10 11s.

Yorkshire's preceptories and estates together were valued at over £1,400. The other twenty-nine counties which produced a Templar income plus those in Wales came to just over £5,600. So Yorkshire was far and away the most valuable county, its nearest rival being Lincolnshire with its five preceptories was valued at just over £900.

Despite King Edward's earlier attempts to protect the British Knights Templar, once their fate was sealed, he needed to decide what would happen to all their property and possessions. Within a month of their arrest, he arranged for all the wool they had owned to be exported, keeping the profit for himself. The following year's fleeces were used as part payment of money he owed. Shortly after the arrests, he sold anything he could lay his hands on that wasn't nailed down.

In 1308, his army in Scotland was on the receiving end of grain harvested from Templar lands and meat and fish from the preceptories were eaten at his coronation feast. In 1312, he sold a lot of timber from their estates which netted him a nice income. On 19 August 1324, the king was deeded Temple Hirst, Temple Newsam and Faxfleet.

Eventually in July 1324 most of the Templar properties were handed over to the Knights Hospitaller, but in spite of a series of papal bulls and litigation on their part, they didn't get all of it. Actually getting possession of what they had been given also proved difficult. All this delay resulted in some of the previously well run, well maintained preceptories and estates falling into ruin.

In Yorkshire, the Hospitallers were given Temple Cowton, Foulbridge, Whitley, Copmanthorpe, Penhill, Westerdale and Ribston with Wetherby. The era of the Knights Templar in Yorkshire had finally come to an end.

APPENDIX I

FAMOUS POPES, KINGS & PEOPLE

The Knights Templar Order was a self perpetuating, growing, living organism. It emerged from a group of nine like-minded knights, spreading to an organisation wielding such power the like of which has never been replicated. However, like all young, growing forms, the newly created Knights Templar Order needed sustenance from the outside world. This came from those in power bases across all Christendom in one shape or another.

Bernard of Clairvaux

Bernard of Clairvaux was born near Dijon France in 1090 and died at Clairvaux France in 1153.

Clairvaux Abbey was founded in 1115 and is situated in a rather uncultivated valley near to a tributary of the Aube River; it was also known as the Vallée d'Absinthe (Valley of Bitterness). Its last abbot died in 1824 and the abbey fell into disrepair, and finally came into the hands of the French State. During restoration, it was decided that it should become a prison; perhaps then an apt name – The Valley of Bitterness!

The abbey was a Cistercian house, an offshoot of the Benedictines. It was there that Bernard became abbot and the abbey became the principal monastery of the sub-Order of Cistercians under the direction of the abbot at Cîteaux. Clairvaux soon became the most significant Cistercian house due to the formidable Bernard; his world soon extended into affairs outside the confines of monastic life. By 1124, when Pope Honorius II was elected, Bernard of Clairvaux was a great churchman. He was included in all the most important religious debates and negotiations; Papal legates sought his guidance and advice. In 1129, he was invited to the synod of Troyes where he rallied to the cause of the Knights Templar. Through him, the Knights Templar had a monastic rule, which in turn led them to become a well ordered and disciplined fighting force; not all crusader armies were efficient by any means. The Knights Templar was set on their way to becoming a great and glorious order.

Bernard of Clairvaux went on to be instrumental in the arbitration between Popes, bishops, kings and countries. For the Knights Templar to have had such an important and well respected spiritual and devout champion who had the ear of Popes and kings, was instrumental in the Order gaining many favours from subsequent monarchs and pontiffs in the years to come.

One should not assume that Bernard had all his own way. There were those who were opposed to the idea of a new order and could not see why one should be established. Moreover, there was jealousy among many who also had the ear of the Pope and felt that Bernard held too much sway in the political arena.

One of the detractors was Cardinal Harmeric who called Bernard 'a noisy troublesome frog'. Bernard, however, had close family ties with the powerful house of Champagne whom the Pope did not want to antagonise. So in the end, Bernard of Clairvaux had his way.

Popes throughout the Knights Templar history

There were thirty-seven Popes from the time of the First Crusade to the time of the dissolution of the Knights Templar Order. Pope Urban II launched the First Crusade about twenty years before the inception of the Knights Templar. During the 200 years of the might of the Order, some Popes were outstanding in their support; others were ambivalent and yet others were opposed. The Knights Templar were responsible only to the Pope and not to any secular or other ecclesiastical authority, therefore no Pope could be indifferent to them. Sometimes three Popes reigned within a year; on occasion, two Popes claimed sovereignty at one time, one in France and one in Italy, at yet other times it seems there is a wide gap between one Pope and the next. These 'vacancies' arose when the process of choosing a new Pope was a lengthy one, often because of the absence of some of the cardinals. The longest break occurred between November 1268 and September 1271 following the death of Pope Clement IV. In order to hurry the process up a bit, the decision was made to lock the cardinals in seclusion until they reached a decision.

Through all the changes, the Knights Templar remained constant to their aims and objectives, ever faithful to their cause.

Urban II (Pope from 1088–99)
The First Crusade was launched by Pope Urban II in 1095.

Paschal II (Pope from 1099–1118)

Gelasius II (Pope from 1118–9)

Calistus II (Pope from 1119–24)
A high born, blue blooded personage, he was dubbed 'the father of peace' by the chroniclers of the time. A spiritual leader, the reign of Calistus II strengthened the policy of the Church. With his firm, powerful character, he was able to effect a settlement between Church and State which resulted in a peaceful coexistence. He made Henry I of England accept the consecrated Bishop Thurstan as Bishop of York.

Most importantly, Calistus II convoked the first Lateran Council in 1123. There were twenty-two disciplinary canons. Canon 16 read: '. . .Against those who molest pilgrims on their way. . .' This Council was attended by almost 300 bishops and 600 abbots and was an emotional event; many documents were signed, reinforcing earlier decrees that previously had only been conciliatory. At the time it was hailed as a new era within the Church.

The Knights Templar had already been formed by this time and though Calistus had little to do with them, he did support them and he paved the way for councils being able to ratify their resolutions. Later this would be to the benefit of the Knights Templar.

Honorius II (Pope from 1124–30)

In contrast to Calistus, Honorius was of lowly birth. He was extremely learned and prior to attaining the position of Pope, he was chosen by no less than three earlier Popes for delicate negotiations. He was called to Rome by Paschal II, he accompanied Gelasius II into exile and in 1119, Calistus II sent him as legate to Henry V, the German Emperor. In 1128, Pope Honorius II granted a papal sanction to the Order known as the Knights Templar declaring them to be the 'Army of God'. He also established the white cloak as the Templars outer garment, which he intended to symbolise their purity of intent.

Innocent II (Pope from 1130–43)

Pope Innocent II issued *Omne Datum Optimum*, a papal bull in 1139 that endorsed the Order of Poor Knights of Christ and of the Temple of Solomon. Thus the Knights Templar Rule was officially approved, and papal protection achieved. This made the Knights Templar a self-governing body and granted them a monetary base for financing their military activities in the Holy Land. They were charged with protecting the Church against all enemies of the True Cross.

Controversially, the *Omne Datum Optimum* bull also promised that all proceeds and plunder from the Muslim conquest went to the Order and, in addition, made the Order free from all taxes and tithes. Not, one imagines, the most popular move by a Pope, however although it was unusual, Pope Innocent's successors would also bring the Knights Templar even more power.

Celestine II (Pope from 1143-4)

Pope Celestine also proved to be rather controversial in his papal bulls. His *Milites Templi*, meaning Soldiers of the Temple, published in 1144, ordered the clergy to protect the Knights Templar and promoted the faithful flock to contribute funds to the Order. It allowed the Templars to make their own collections once a year even in areas under interdict, a penalty that temporarily bans a specific person or group from receiving the sacraments.

Lucius II (Pope from 1144–5)

Eugene III (Pope from 1145–53)

Pope Eugene issued a controversial bull. It was the *Militia Dei* which means 'Soldiers of God'. This bull gave independence from the local clerical hierarchy by providing the Order with the right to take tithes and burial fees and to bury their dead in their own cemeteries. Therefore, it confirmed and cemented the previous two papal bulls, thereby forming and establishing a bedrock for the future wealth and achievement of the Order.

It was also at this time that Eugene III had the Order sew on the red crosses on the left breast of their tunics and the shoulder of their mantles to distinguish themselves from others by symbolising their willingness to shed blood and die for the faith.

Anastasius IV (Pope from 1153–4)

Adrian IV (Pope from 1154–9)

Alexander III (Pope from 1159–81)
In 1163, the '*Retrais et etablissements de Temple*' was added to the Rule. This was an extra 675 articles covering etiquette and formality of life, characterizing the hierarchical status, regulating the chapters, settling punishment and penance and changes to the election of the Grand Master. Pope Alexander III issued a bull recognising the amended rules. In addition, the motto '*Non nobis, Domine, non nobis sednomini tuo da gloriam*' was inscribed on the black and white standard of the Knights Templar. Their seal showed two men on horseback. There have been many guesses as to what two riders on horseback could mean. The best guess is that it symbolised the Templar as both a soldier and a pilgrim.

Lucius III (Pope from 1181–5)

Urban III (Pope from 1185–7)

Gregory VIII (Pope in 1187)

Clement III (Pope from 1187–91)

Celestine III (Pope from 1191–8)

Innocent III (pope from 1198–1216)
Not all was sweetness and light between the various Popes and the Templar Order. In 1207, Pope Innocent III wrote a bull condemning pride among the Templars and reminding them of their vows of chastity and poverty.

Honorius III (Pope from 1216–27)

Gregory IX (Pope from 1227–41)

Celestine IV (Pope in 1241)

Innocent IV (Pope from 1243–54)

Alexander IV (Pope from 1254–61)

Urban IV (Pope from 1261–4)

Clement IV (Pope from 1265–8)

Gregory X (Pope from 1271–6)
Pope Gregory X was not the most popular Pope in Britain. In 1275, he levied a heavy tax burden that concerned all and sundry in Britain. The tax demanded one tenth of the value of property including that which belonged to the clergy. All, that is, except that of the Military Orders. The tax collectors took an oath of honesty at the Temple Church and the accumulation of this tax, a vast sum, was delivered to the Temple church for protection and security.

Innocent V (Pope in 1276)

Adrian V (Pope in 1276)

John XXI (Pope from 1276–7)

Nicholas III (Pope from 1277–80)

Martin IV (Pope from 1281–5)

Honorius IV (Pope from 1285–7)

Nicholas IV (Pope from 1288–92)
In 1291 after the fall of Acre, Pope Nicholas tried very hard to amalgamate the Knights Templar and the Knights Hospitallers into one order. This however, was strongly resisted by the Grand Master of the Templars and the idea was quickly buried.

St Celestine V (Pope in 1294)

Boniface VIII (Pope from 1294–1303)
A papal bull was issued by Pope Boniface VIII that enabled the Templars to have a tax-free status on exports and imports to and from Cyprus.

Benedict XI (Pope from 1303–4)

Clement V (Pope from 1305–14)
In 1265, Clement V wrote to the Order asking them to show greater humility in the face of the Church. The Knights Templar were still under the protection of the Holy See which did not want to hear accusations of arrogance against them. These accusations and objections were quite possibly the forerunner of the later open

allegations and indictments to the Pope by King Philip of France. In 1312, Clement V finally crushed the Knights Templar at the Council of Vienne with the papal bull, *Vox in Excelso*.

English kings throughout the Knights Templar history

King Henry I
Henry I was born 1068 at Selby Abbey, was sovereign from 1100 and died 1135 at St Denis-le-Fermont, interred at Reading Abbey.

King Henry I was, in a sense, instrumental in bringing the Knights Templar Order to Britain. Hugh de Payen visited Normandy in 1128 and was received by Henry. He heaped gifts of silver and gold on Hugh, together with privileges and accolades. Henry also supported Hugh's aims to travel to Britain in order to encourage a British arm of the Knights Templar. It is unclear if a Templar establishment was actually instituted at this time though it is most likely that it was.

King Stephen
Stephen was born 1096 at Blois France, sovereign from 1135 and died 1154 at Dover Castle.

King Stephen was crowned king of England in 1135 in London; by 1130 he was already the richest man in England and Normandy. The grandson of William the Conquer, his reign was one of disappointment to his people. His virtue, in a sense, saw his downfall.

The Anglo-Saxon Chronicle says of him that during his reign there was:

> . . . nothing but strife, evil and robbery . . . the traitors saw that Stephen was a good-humoured, kindly, and easy-going man who inflicted no punishment, then they committed all manner of horrible crimes . . . And so it lasted for nineteen years while Stephen was King, till the land was all undone and darkened with such deeds, and men said openly that Christ and his angels slept.

Yet, this is the king who gave the first notable grants of land to the Templars. The king and his wife were exceptionally generous; it has to be said, so was Matilda, his rival for the throne. Among other lands, Stephen bestowed the manor of Snainton in North Yorkshire to them. He gave it on condition they 'find a chaplain to celebrate divine service daily and to receive and entertain poor guests and pilgrims there, and to bring and blow the horn at dusk every night, lest pilgrims and strangers should lose their way.'

Not only did Stephen settle land to the Knights Templar Order, he also accorded them privileges, which was to help them gather much wealth for the Order as a whole and set a pattern for future kings and Popes. Through Stephen's benevolence, the Temple's English star was on the rise, it was to become a firm foundation on which much of the Knights Templar wealth was built.

King Henry II

Henry II was born 1133 at Le Mans, France, sovereign from 1154 and died 1189 in Chinon, France.

King Henry II has the reputation of having been the greatest of the medieval kings. It is true to say, in modern parlance, he was able to see the big picture. He often acted as a mediator between both Spanish and French kings and was essentially a peacemaker and a man of peace.

After the turbulence and lawlessness of Stephen's reign, he realised that the welfare of the nation was the most effective way of assuring and underpinning his own power. He reined in the errant barons and refined the Norman administration by creating a competent system of government. A major legacy from Henry was his achievement in the development of a structured justice system. Together with Ranulf de Glanvill, he established a royal judicial court, rather than the feudal and private system. Procedural advances included the greatly extended use of writs and twelve-man juries. The list of Henry's religious foundations is quite considerable, including gifts to the Knights Templar. In 1188, the Saladin tithe and Scutage tax were levied on those who did not take up the Cross, which marked a new era in the history of taxation in England. These taxes demonstrated his genuine interest in the crusades.

The blot on Henry's landscape was the conflict with Thomas Becket. This antagonism with Becket effectively began with a dispute over whether the secular courts could try clergy who had committed a secular offence. It ended with the death of Thomas Becket.

After Becket's death, there were still Church courts and the clergy could appeal to Rome if they didn't agree with a royal verdict. This continued for the next 300 years. As part of his penance, King Henry agreed to send money to the crusader states. The Knights Templar guarded this money until King Henry either made a pilgrimage or went on a crusade. Henry delayed his crusade for many years and in the end, never went at all, despite a visit to him by Patriarch Heraclius of Jerusalem in 1184, offering him the crown of the Kingdom of Jerusalem. Henry II possibly owned one ship commanded by Alan Trenchemer which was loaned to the Knights Templar. The Order was also given the advowson of St Clement Danes, a church which is in the City of Westminster in London.

Full of energy, fired with ambition and highly intelligent, King Henry settled his lands – until his sons intervened.

King Richard I

Richard I was born in 1157 at Oxford, sovereign from 1189 and died in 1199 in Limousin, France.

What can one say about Richard I? Together with the Templars, legend and myth entwined his life. Known as Richard the Lionheart, he was above average in height with a shock of red hair which made him stand out from the crowd. Some think of him as the great crusader, valiant and fearsome. Others think of him as a neglectful king, spending only a few months of his ten-year reign in England and emptying the financial coffers for the crusades.

However, upon his return from the crusades, King Richard confirmed the Templars land holdings. He also granted them exemption from all road tolls, pleas, taxes known as Danegeld, which was a levy to pay off, in particular, Viking raiders so land was not razed and ransacked. He also granted the Templars discharge from the levy which compelled a parish or manor to pay for a death 'in secret', in other words, a murder of an unknown man, since an unknown man was considered to be a Norman. This tax was a hangover from the time of King Canute; the origin of the dead man was merely changed from a Dane to a Norman.

Not all the Templars were of high repute; there is at least one instance where greed overcame piety and the rule of 'forsaking worldly goods'! In 1188, Walter of Coventry, a monk and chronicler connected to a religious house in York, told a story of a Knight Templar named Gilbert de Ogrestan. He was accused of misappropriating taxes collected for the Saladin tithe. He was, as can be imagined, very harshly punished by his preceptor.

Richard was buried at Fontevraud Abbey in France alongside his father, or rather, bits of him were, as parts of his body were buried in three different places – the majority, though, at Fontevraud.

King John

John was born in 1167 at Oxford, sovereign from 1199 and died 1216 in Newark. King John had considerable dealings with the Knights Templar; financial transactions figured strongly as John beggared the Crown's finances. John was resident at the London Temple when the barons first made their demands upon him which led to the famous Runnymede declaration of Magna Carta to which Aymeric de St Maur, Master of the Temple in England, was a signatory (*see* chapter 10).

King John presented lands to the Templars for their support in this matter, including land in Yorkshire.

Apart from the barons, John was not popular with the Church either; he fell out with the Pope in 1207 for squabbling about who should be Archbishop of Canterbury. The Pope excommunicated him and put England under Church law, which was terrible for the people. In the end, John had to accede to the wishes of the Pope.

John should be given some credit, though, for having the forsight to instigate a navy for England. In 1203, John ordered that all shipyards in England should furnish at least one ship for the new shipyard at Portsmouth. By 1204 he had forty-five ships available with three or four new ships each year. The Knights Templar under Richard I had demonstrated the advantages of a standing fleet insomuch that ships had been deployed to support his army in the coastal route march from Acre to Jaffa. John also created an admiralty with four admirals.

Another major tradition King John started was that of banking with the Temple, this was of enormous benefit for the Templar Order.

King Henry III

Henry III was born 1207 at Winchester, sovereign from 1216 and died at Westminster in 1272.

Henry also had dealings with the Knights Templar on a number of levels. He entrusted them with diplomatic, military and above all, financial missions. As a king, he was quite generous to the Order, bequeathing manors and assarts and granting them money and various gifts in the form of food and wine.

At one time he considered being buried at the London Temple; however, finally he was buried at Westminster Abbey which was fitting, since he had spent time and much money on the rebuilding of it in the Gothic manner.

King Edward I

Edward I was born in 1239 at Westminster, sovereign from 1272 and died in 1307 at Burgh-on-Sands

King Edward I was also known as 'Edward Longshanks' due to being tall, as 'Edward the Lawgiver' because of his legal reforms, and as 'Hammer of the Scots' for his attempts to conquer Scotland. He intended to be known as Edward IV, in deference to the three earlier Saxon kings, but this did not come about and so began the renumbering of the English Edwards.

Prior to his accession to the throne, the then Prince Edward I took part in the Ninth Crusade, also known as 'The Crusade of Edward of England'. Its aim was to relieve the besieged Christian city of Acre. Edward made a daring raid on the city of Ququn, captured Nazareth and fought a number of other minor battles, all of which gave a much needed morale lift to Edward's small army. Eventually, this resulted in a ten-year treaty being signed which held for the full ten years. Edward's reputation was strengthened by his involvement and participation at Acre. During his time in the Holy Land, Prince Edward was attacked by an assassin who was able to stab him in the arm before the Prince could kill him. Poison from the knife gradually flooded along his arm and into his torso; little hope was held for his survival. His continued existence is due to two factors: first, the surgeon, not knowing what to do, decided to cut away the flesh that had turned black, which was an enormous help. Equally, the Master of the Knights Templar, Thomas Bérard, sent healing drugs to help cleanse the body.

Assassins were rooted in the breakaway Islamic Shias, dating from the time of Mohammed and then from a further breakaway group, the Ismailis. Within this sect, a dedicated core of killers was founded known as the Assassins. To this day, political murders are described as an 'assassination'. When King Richard I had had a visit from an assassin during his time in the Holy Land, a poisoned knife was merely left on his pillow as a warning

It was at this time that Edward received word that his father had died. The English Council met at the Temple in London and drafted a letter to Prince Edward informing him of his accession to the throne. Edward left the war and the Holy Land to claim his throne. He landed in England in 1274, after four years away, to a tumultuous welcome. At the time, the Knights Templar still held political importance; however, this was to change under the reign of King Edward I.

Edward took a keen interest in understanding the way in which his government worked. He made reforms to regain royal control in government and administration and among other things, Parliament began to meet regularly. Although still quite limited to matters of taxation, it enabled Edward I to obtain a number of taxation grants which had been impossible for Henry III. His reign is marked by his desire to obtain a degree of cooperation between the Crown and the population. He genuinely had the welfare of his people close to his heart. He was mainly responsible for the redesigning of the Tower of London as we see it today, including the infamous Traitors' Gate.

At this time, the Knights Templar influence was on the wane. With King Edward I, they had a much reduced role in all levels of affairs. Financial discharge was handled by Italian merchants and diplomacy was undertaken by mendicant orders. In 1283, Edward was bold enough to raid the treasury at the London Temple. Giving the reason for entering as to remove his mother's jewels, he plundered the treasury and removed his hoard to the Tower of London.

He died on his way to war with the Scottish Robert the Bruce; he lay in State in a tiny twelfth-century village church until his body was finally taken for burial at Westminster Abbey.

King Edward II

Edward II was born in 1284 in Caernarfon, sovereign from 1308 and died at Berkeley Castle in 1327

Edward was the first English prince to be granted the title of Prince of Wales, conferred on him by his father in 1301. He was the fourth son and unlikely to become king; however, his three elder brothers died and the least equipped son became heir to the throne. His reign was fraught with antipathy towards him by his barons because of his homosexuality and his giving power to his favourite male friends, first Gaveston and then Despencer. He was extravagant; his military endeavours in Scotland were a disaster and were singularly unpopular.

On the other hand, he was the first sovereign to create colleges in the universities of Oxford and Cambridge, Oriel and Kings Hall respectively.

Within the world of the Templars, he is best known for his handling of the Templar dissolution (*see* chapter 12). When he first received word from King Philip of France that he should round-up the Templars and continue with their dissolution, Edward did not accede to his wishes, in fact, he wrote to other kings and to the Pope in their defence. He could not believe they were guilty of the accusations levelled against them. These accusations ranged from heresy – renouncing Christ and spitting on the cross, to homosexuality. There had been confessions obtained in France under torture and were therefore unreliable. King Edward eventually capitulated, having received a papal bull from Pope Clement V which left him no choice but to adhere to the request.

Some Templar benefactors

Hugh Bigod

Hugh was born in 1095 at Belvoir Castle, Leicestershire and died 1176 or 1177, possibly in Palestine. He was connected with Foulbridge.

Hugh was the second son of Roger Bigod and inherited his lands in Yorkshire from his maternal uncle, Berengar de Tosny.

Hugh was definitely a man with his eye on the main chance. He always liked to be on the winning side which led to him frequently changing his allegiance and breaking promises. Consequently, he has gone down in history as treacherous, conniving and unreliable.

He was made Earl of Norfolk by King Stephen, whom he had helped to gain the English crown. Then Matilda entered the arena and he decided to support her efforts to acquire the throne. She ultimately had to return to France when her major supporter and half-brother, Robert of Gloucester, died. By then, Hugh was again backing Stephen, who was surprisingly lenient with his rebellious subject. But in 1148 when Stephen and the Archbishop of Canterbury fell out, Bigod sided with the Archbishop; he was later reconciled with the king yet again.

Five years passed before Hugh swapped sides once more, this time hitching his star to the fortunes of the man who would shortly become Henry II. But Henry's leadership style, with its introduction of laws which gave England a more ordered judicial system, did not suit Hugh at all. So insurrection became his personal order of the day. Henry was a much stronger monarch than Stephen had been and in 1157, he quelled Hugh's little rebellion.

All was quiet until 1173 when three of Henry's sons led a revolt against him, which in turn led to a year-long civil war in England. Needless to say, Hugh Bigod was right there – on the side of the rebels and their lost cause. This time he did not get away scot free and had to forfeit his castles as punishment, but Henry allowed him to keep his earldom and his lands.

Hugh died a few short years later. It is thought he was in Palestine at the time which gives rise to some uncertainty about the actual date of his death. Generally it is given as 1177, but on 1 March 1177, his son, Roger, appealed to the king in his father's absence, to settle a dispute with his stepmother (Hugh had married twice). If Hugh had indeed died in Palestine, it would have taken some time for the news to reach England, so he may well have died the year before. Unless, of course, he died in England. So even in death, this colourful character still caused problems!

Roger de Mowbray

Roger was born in 1119 in Lincolnshire and died in1188 in the Holy Land. He had connections with Penhill, Temple Cowton, Faxfleet and bestowed various other gifts.

Roger de Mowbray started his military career at the Battle of the Standard at the age of nineteen and seemed to fight his way through life until he was captured at the Battle of Hattin at sixty-eight years of age.

His father was Nigel d'Aubigny (Albini) who had divorced his first wife on grounds of co-sanguinity and married Roger's mother. He was justly described as 'one of the most favoured of Henry's 'new men.' Indeed, it was Henry I who conferred the change of surname on young Roger d'Aubigny who, at nine years of age, took over the honour and name of Mowbray. The largest and most important estates in the country were known as 'honours', which says something about what this young boy received.

Early in the morning of 22 August 1138, the nineteen-year-old teenager engaged in his first major battle just outside Northallerton where, according to Aelred of

Rievaulx, he did well. The Battle of the Standard only lasted two hours, but it apparently gave the youngster a taste for fighting because three years later, he was at it again. He joined King Stephen's forces who were besieging Lincoln in 1141, but this time his luck was out. Along with the king and other nobles, Roger was captured and lost some of his lands to his captors, Ranulf, Earl of Chester and William Romaine.

In 1148 – the year the Templars adopted the eight-pointed red cross on their white mantles – Roger joined the Second Crusade and went off to the Holy Land. When he got back, he successfully regained both his lost lands and the honour of Mowbray. Then, like Hugh Bigod, he joined the ill-fated rebellion against Henry II which resulted in him losing more land and castles.

Now in his late fifties, he decided to go on pilgrimage to the Holy Land. When he came home, he left again almost immediately, but as a soldier once more. He fought at the Battle of Hattin but again found himself taken prisoner, this time by the Saracens. He had been extremely generous to the Knights Templar during his lifetime and so it comes as no surprise to learn that they paid the ransom demanded for him.

Unfortunately, he died quite soon afterwards and was buried in the Holy Land. Or was he? Legend has it that he returned to England after his release, didn't die for another fifteen years and was buried with his mother at Byland Abbey in North Yorkshire. This story may have come about because the monks there wanted some sort of memorial to Roger de Mowbray as he had founded their abbey. So what was taken to be his grave in later centuries was probably simply a monument to his memory.

The de Lacey Family
The de Lacey family (also spelt Lascy, Lacie, Laci and Lacy) were connected with Temple Newsam, primarily Henry de Lacey, but the family had such close connections with Yorkshire that the first few generations are all well worth a mention.

The family originally came from Calvados in France. However, Walter de Lacey and his son Ilbert decided to support William the Conqueror's claim to the English crown. They fought with him at the Battle of Hastings and took a major role in the subsequent conquest of the country. Walter was said to have been a very close companion of William's and it was observed at the time that nobody was rewarded with more possessions and favours than the de Laceys.

The family was given vast estates in Yorkshire and elsewhere. In fact, they were given so much that their holdings in Yorkshire alone covered seven pages of the Domesday Book. Ilbert proceeded to build a fine castle at Pontefract in the late 1080s from whence he controlled his lands. They broadened their influence to such an extent that Ilbert's son, Robert was given the honour of Clitheroe in Lancashire.

Ilbert's grandson was the Henry de Lacey whose connection with Temple Newsam has been previously discussed. He also founded Kirkstall Abbey in Leeds, moving it from its original site to its present position which he considered to be nicer. He went on crusade and died in the Holy Land.

In 1193, the castle and the honour passed to Roger de Lacy who was present at the signing of the Magna Carta.

Ralph de Hastings

Ralph de Hastings was connected with Temple Hirst, but the most interesting bit of information about this benefactor is his relationship to the Master of the Temple in England. It was his brother, Richard de Hastings, who held office from 1155–64.

When Henry II ascended the throne, he soon recognised Richard's value and used him in various important negotiations. Along with two other Knights Templar, Richard was also a witness to the marriage between the infant daughter of the king of France and Henry's infant son. Fortresses at Gizors near Paris and other places formed part of the little girl's dowry and it was stipulated that these should be consigned to the care of the Templars. However, immediately after the ceremony they handed these dowry items over to King Henry. The French king was not best pleased, but from the terms of the treaty, it would appear that the Templars acted in good faith.

Richard also tried hard to resolve the problems between Thomas Becket and his sovereign, but in this he was unsuccessful.

Robert de Ros (also spelt Roos)

Robert was born in 1177 and died in 1226 and was connected with Ribston and Wetherby.

This family originally had a connection with East Yorkshire as it's thought that the surname was adopted from the Lordship of Ros in Holderness, where they lived. There was also a link with Helmesley in North Yorkshire. William l'Espec had built a castle there which passed to his sister on his death. His sister married Peter de Ros, Robert's great-grandfather and thus the castle found its way into that family's ownership. Robert de Ros had the castle rebuilt some time after 1186 and the keep can still be visited today.

When Robert was fourteen, he paid 1,000 marks to King Richard for what has been described as a 'fine for livery of his lands'. This was simply a payment enabling him to obtain possession of his inherited lands which the king currently held.

Like so many Templar benefactors, Robert seems to have had a bit of a chequered career. In 1197, the twenty-year-old was arrested for an unspecified offence while serving King Richard in France. One Hugh de Chaumont took custody of him, passed him on to William de Spiney for safe keeping at Bonville Castle, but William allowed Robert to escape. King Richard responded by hanging de Spiney and fining de Chaumont 1,200 marks, on payment of which young Robert was allowed to remain free.

Things improved for Robert once King John came to the throne. He was given a barony which had originally belonged to his great-grandmother's father. Then around 1213, he decided to become a monk and his entire barony was given to Philip de Ulcote. The clerical life obviously didn't suit him because in less than a year he gave it up and became Sheriff of Cumberland.

Shortly after that, the power struggle between the barons and King John began in earnest. Initially Robert supported the king, which resulted in some important grants and the governorship of Carlisle. But just as he changed his mind about being a monk, so he also changed his mind about backing King John, and instead embraced the barons' cause.

Stained glass window in the Templar chapel at Ribston, showing the Ros coat of arms with three water 'bottles' which, attached to a yoke, would have been used to carry water to soldiers. (Courtesy of Simon Brighton)

Shortly after the accession of Henry III, Robert's manors were restored to him and he remained in the king's good books until his death in 1226. Some sources think he was buried in the Temple, London where his effigy is still to be seen, but others feel it is more likely to be a later member of the family.

William Greenfield

William was consecrated Archbishop of York in 1306 and died 6 December 1315.

It was William Greenfield who oversaw the trials of the Yorkshire Templars. His education at Oxford was paid for by his predecessor and relative, Archbishop Giffard. He was a much respected statesman whose service to the State was greatly valued by King Edward I. In 1302, he became Chancellor of England for a period of three years before becoming Archbishop of York.

Although William had been chosen for his new responsibilities in December 1304, it was January 1306 before he was consecrated by Pope Clement V. The involvement in the downfall of the Templars by both these clerics is documented in chapter 12.

Archbishop Greenfield died on 6 December 1315 at his palace in Cawood, just North of Selby. He is buried in the north transept of York Minster, where his monument can still be seen.

APPENDIX II

TEMPLAR & MEDIEVAL MISCELLANY

Non nobis Doine,non nobis,
Sed Nomine Tua da gloriam

(Not to us, Lord, not to us,
But to Thy name give the glory)

The battle cry of the Knights Templar

The Templar legacy

It is a little known fact that the last crusade was in fact in the nineteenth century. In 1890, a Brother from the White Fathers of the Sahara petitioned the Pope for a crusade to help stamp out slavery. He wanted about sixty men who would fight to the death but with the chivalry of knights; he was inundated with thousands of applications. The initiative lasted about two years.

Many places still bear remnants of Templar occupation; in Bingley there are finials; in Cottingley there are date stones; and in Halifax there are a couple of double-armed crosses as there are in Leeds, to name a few.

Various works refer to Newland Preceptory near Wakefield as being a Knights Templar preceptory. In fact, it was never a Templar holding, it always belonged to the Knights Hospitaller. The mistake probably arose because the Templars did have property at Newland in Sussex. However, the land at Ravensknowle near Huddersfield may well have belonged to the Knights Templar. In 2006, some rare documents were put up for auction at Bonhams. These included some 'deeds of gift' which came from Temple Newsam and concerned vast tracts of land, mainly in the Huddersfield area.

When the Countess of Albermarle allowed the Templars permission to run their greyhounds through her property at Dunnington near Bridlington and Holderness near Hull, it had to be within sight of her warrener, who was like a game keeper of today.

Knights Templar emblem over a gateway.

Franchises

Franchises are not a new phenomenon; in the Middle Ages franchises were awarded to the Knights Templars, Knights Hospitaller and to the Church, among others. In York, the archbishop was the principle holder of franchises. The main one was that the Church took the third penny of income from the city's tolls but was given control or the franchise of the Foss Bridge. There was also the 'bishopshire', which was the area around York Minster. The archbishop held the power of judicial administrator for all minor offences which happened in and around the Minster. This was a franchise bestowed in order to help raise revenues for the Church.

The Templar cross

St George was hijacked as the crusader knight in much the same way as St James was for the Spanish. The red cross of St George was in fact the red cross of the crusaders.

The Templar cross is an international symbol for healing – the International Red Cross and has also been adapted to encompass Muslim culture through the Red Crescent Movement.

The Templar cross is the main feature of the coat of arms of London where it is shown with the tapered sword of the Templars.

The Inner and Middle Temple used by Lawyers in London was originally Knights Templar land and is where their famous Temple Church is located.

Friday the thirteenth

Friday 13 October 1307 was not a good day for any Knight Templar living in France. Most, if not all, the Templars in that country were arrested in a well co-ordinated exercise masterminded by Philip IV. So among other legacies we have from the Templars, any Friday which falls on the thirteenth of the month is considered by many to be unlucky.

Medieval customs & practices

Slavery

According to Giraldus Cambrenisis, William the Conqueror found slaves were being sold in the north of England and in the west at Bristol. The king therefore bought in laws to stop the practice. However, a hundred years later, the slave trade was still being carried on, in spite of the king's order. It was not a blanket law. Point 41 says:

> . . . Also we forbid anyone to sell a Christian into foreign lands and especially to heathens. For let great care be taken lest their souls for which Christ gave his life be sold into damnation. . . And we prohibit any one to sell a man out of the country. But if he who wishes to make his serf free, hand him over to the Sheriff by his right hand in full assembly, he must proclaim him quit of the yoke of his servitude by manumission, and show him free ways and gates and give him arms – a lance and a sword; finally the man is made free. . .

Incidentally, if a serf ran away from his lord, in order to remain free, he had to go to a nearby town and remain living free for one year and a day.

Marriage

Medieval marriage was very firmly the province of the Church and the sacrament of marriage was central to Christian doctrine. Marriage laws began to evolve in the Middle Ages; the Council of Westminster decreed that no man shall give his daughter or female relative without a priestly blessing. Later, councils declared that marriages should be open affairs and not conducted in secret.

There was no divorce but marriages could be annulled if it was deemed that the couple were too closely related.

Noble weddings could take place in a castle, providing the union had a blessing in a church later. Country weddings were quite different; usually the ceremony was in a church performed by the local priest. In outlaying districts, the wedding day would have to coincide with a visit by the priest. It is from the country wedding that we can trace some surviving customs. Villagers would shower the couple with seed or grain to ensure a fruitful union; the forerunner of confetti. The groom would provide a broken coin; he and his bride each keeping one part instead of having a ring which may have been too expensive for him to purchase.

The tiered wedding cake of today is rooted in a medieval custom. At the wedding feast, each person bought with them some small cakes; these would be piled up on top of each other without falling over. The bride and groom would then kiss across the top of them for good luck and prosperity. Much later the cakes were covered with icing sugar which gradually progressed into the tiered cake of today.

A blue dress was then a symbol of purity; both the bride and groom would wear blue ribbons attached to their clothing. Hence the wedding rhyme includes 'something blue'. Garters are also a leftover from the medieval bride.

Returning crusaders brought back the Saracen tradition of weaving orange blossom into a crown wreath. The blossoms were expensive, so were only seen in noble marriages as befitting a knight.

Christmas

The pagan tradition of burning the Yuletide log is carried on today under the guise of a cake. The Yule log was burned over the Christmas period but part of it was kept to use the following year to light a new log. The word 'yule' is derived from the word 'iul' which means 'wheel of the year or the repeated pattern of time'. Many of us have a Yule-log cake at Christmas time; a repeated pattern each year.

Another tradition we are familiar with is the punch that is often offered at the festive time of year. This is derived from a strong drink made of ale, honey and spices. A host greeted visitors with this drink in a bowl; he would lift the bowl to drink and greet his visitors with the words *waes hael* – 'be well' or 'good health'; the visitors then repeated the greeting in a similar fashion.

Mince pies are a familiar sight as the Christmas season draws near. Originally cooked in an oblong shape to represent the crib of Jesus, they contained shredded meat. It was important to add three spices: cinnamon, cloves and nutmeg to represent the three gifts given to Jesus. It was thought lucky to eat a pie a day over the twelve days of Christmas. Perhaps the peasants thought it lucky to have that much food!

In the Middle Ages, the Church would have decorated a tree with apples on Christmas Eve which they called 'Adam and Eve night'. The trees were always kept inside.

Holly, ivy and mistletoe had been of great importance since the time of the Druids; Christians believed that all the berries had been white and that they turned red when Christ was made to wear a crown of thorns. Ivy was not originally allowed inside the church as it had associations with the Roman god, Bacchus. Later in the Middle Ages, it was allowed in church as it was then thought to help to recognise witches and to protect against the plague.

Christmas owes much of its popularity in medieval times to the liturgical dramas untaken by the Church. There are remnants of eleventh- and twelfth-century manuscripts called topiaries which were stories of the Magi and the adoration of the shepherds. As the presentation grew in scale, the characters became too profane for the Church which eventually banned the performances in churches. In taking on a secular role, the religious dramas evolved into the mystery plays. Mumming was the forerunner of today's Christmas pantomime.

We are all familiar with the word crèche and what it means today. However, a crèche meant a display in church of the nativity, with angels shepherds and the Magi as well as the Holy family.

Other medieval miscellany

Vital statistics
A common misconception is that of the height of men in the Middle Ages. The average male was 5ft 7in or 5ft 8in; not that much smaller than today.

People also lived longer than might be supposed. There was a high child mortality rate but if a person lived beyond their teenage years, and barring an awful disease, they could expect to live to around sixty years. Certainly some people did reach seventy or even eighty years old.

Innovations
We are inclined to think that in the Middle Ages people thought the world was flat; far from it, they were well aware that the world is round.

Among things invented in the Middle Ages were wheelbarrows, windmills, guns, glasses, clocks and printing presses.

Humble pie
Numbles was a pie made from the heart, liver, kidneys and brains of the deer for the servants. The best and choicest cuts were reserved for the table of a wealthy family; thus the saying 'to eat humble pie'. It had become 'umble pie' by the fifteenth century and only comparatively recently did 'numbles/umble' finally mutate into 'humble'.

Weights & Measures
All English pounds were divided into 240 pence which remained the case until 1971 when decimalisation came in to being. There were lots of different names for coinage, including groat, mark, shilling and pence.

Many medieval weights and measures are still use to this day. Small measures were based on the human body like the thumb which measured an inch, with twelve of them to a foot. An inch was also measured by the length of three barley corns. Britain began the change from Imperial weights and measures to metrication in 1965 and despite continued pressure from the EU, the two methods continue to run side by side. We are still able to buy a metre of material at 36in wide!

BIBLIOGRAPHY

BOOKS

Ball, Ann, *1185 Inquest : Translation on CD*, Lincolnshire, South Witham
  Archaeology Group, 2007
Barber, Malcolm, *The New Knighthood*, Cambridge, Cambridge University Press, 1995
Brighton, Simon, *In Search of the Knights Templar*, London, Weidenfeld &
  Nicholson, 2006
Brown, Allen, *History of the Kings Works*, Colvin & Taylor, HMSO, 1963
Burke, John, *A Genealogical and Heraldic History of the Commoners of Great
  Britain and Ireland in Four Volumes,* , Clearfield Co., 1998
Cantor, Norman F., *Medieval History: The Life and Death of a Civilization*, New
  York, MacMillan, 1963
Daniell, Christopher, *Death & Burial in Medieval England 1066–1550*, Routledge, 1998
Darwin, Sir Francis, *The Pipe and Tabor An Address to a Society of Morris
  Dancers*, Oxford, 1914
Dixon, William Henry, *Fasti Eboracenses: Lives of the Archbishops of York*,
  London, Longman, Gree, Longman and Roberts, 1863.
Dugdale, W., ed., *Monasticon Anglicanum*, London, Longman, Hurst, Rees, Orme
  and Brown, 1830
Gardiner, Laurence, *Bloodline of the Holy Grail*, Beverley, Fair Winds Press, 2002
Hall, J.G., *Cave Castle*, Hull, Edwin Ombler, 1892
Hammond, Peter, *Food and Feast in Medieval England*, Stroud, Sutton, 2005
Hibbert, Christopher, *The English: A Social History 1066–1945*, Grafton, 1987
Hilliam, David, *Kings, Queens, Bones and Bastards*, Stroud, Sutton, 2004
Kealey, Edward J., *Harvesting the Air: Windmill Pioneers in Twelfth Century
  England*, University of California Press, 1992
Knight, Christopher & Lomas, Robert, *The Hiram Key*, London, Arrow Books, 2006
Lord, Evelyn, *The Knights Templar in Britain,* Harlow, Pearson Education Ltd, 2004
Mills, A.D., *A Dictionary of English Place-names*, Oxford, Oxford University
  Press, 1991
Neave, Susan, *Medieval Parks of East Yorkshire*, Hull, Hutton Press, 1991
Nicholson, Helen J., *Knight Templar 1120–1312*, Oxford, Osprey, 2004
    Translation of 'The downfall of the Templars and a letter in their defence' from
    Cheney, C.R. *Medieval Texts and Studies* Oxford, Oxford University Press, 1973
Nutt family, *The Story of Foulbridge*, privately published, nd.

Olsen, Oddvar, ed., *The Templar Papers*, Franklin Lakes, New Page Books, 2006

Power, Eileen, *Medieval Women*, Cambridge, Cambridge University Press, 1975

Ralls, Karen, *The Templars and the Grail*, Wheaton, Quest Books, 2003

Reader, Eleanor M., *Broomfleet & Faxfleet*, York, William Sessions, 1972

Rowling, Marjorie, *Life in Medieval Times*, Pedigree Books, 1970

Salzmann, L.F. *Henry II*, Boston, Mifflin, 1914

Tull, George F.*Traces of the Templars*, Rotheram, The King's England Press, 2000

Unwin, Robert. *Wetherby – The History of a Yorkshire Market Town*, Leeds, Leeds University Press, 1987

Wallace-Murphy, Tim & Hopkins, Marilyn. *Rosslyn Guardian of Secrets of the Holy Grail*, Element Books, 1999

Warren, W.L. *Henry II*, Yale University Press, 2000

Worsfold, Revd J.N. *The History of Haddlesey*, E Stock, England, 1894

PERIODICALS & PRINTED PUBLICATIONS

Bennett, Mattew, 'La Régle du Temple as a Military Manual or How to Deliver a Cavalry Charge', *Studies in Medieval History*, 1989

Dafoe, Stephen, 'The Fall of Acre: The Last Battle for the Holy Land', *Templar History Magazine*, vol. 1, no. 2, Winter 2002

Egan, Geoff, 'Miniature Toys of Childhood', *British Archaeology*, Issue 35

Hamilton, Bernard, 'Spreading the Gospel in the Middle Ages', *History Today*, vol. 53–1

Land, Pip, 'The Burning of Bartle', *Dalesman Magazine*, August 2003

Leyburn Tourist Information Centre, 'The Bartle Trail, West Witton leaflet'

Orme, Nicholas, 'Child's Play in Medieval England', *History Today*, vol. 51–10

Otto, Beatrice K, 'Fools Are Everywhere', *History Today*, vol. 51–6

Owen, James, 'Mudlarks', *National Geographic*, May 2004

Perkins, Clarence, 'The Wealth of the Knights Templars in England and the Disposition of it after their Dissolution', *American Historical Review*, vol. 15, no. 2, 1910

Williams, Michael, 'The History of Deforestation' *History Today*, vol. 51–7

ONLINE ARTICLES

Arkenberg, J.S., ed., 'Guide to Medieval Terms', http://the-orb.net

Bedford, Philip, 'General History About Bells and Handbells', www.handbells.org

Birrell, Jean, 'Peasant Craftsmen in the Medieval Forest, www.bahs.org.uk

Bonney, Margaret, 'The English medieval wool and cloth trade: new approaches for the local historian', British Association for Local History, www.le.ac.uk

Bradley, Raymond S., 'Climate of the Last Millenium', www. stephenschneider.stanford.edu

Campbell, Bruce M.S., 'Changing perspectives on medieval English agriculture', www.neha.nl

Britnell, Richard, 'The marketing of grain in England, 1250–1350' www.dur.ac.uk

Gans, Paul J., Various articles on medieval technology, http://scholar.chem.nyu.edu

Green, Judith A., 'The Descent of Belvoir', http://users.ox.ac.uk

Hanson, Caleb, 'The Fairs of Champagne', www.dragonbear.com

Hoggard, Brian, 'Knights of the Temple (Part 1)', www.whitedragon.org

Jackson, Don, 'History of Whitkirk', www.btinternet.com/~whitkirk/history

Karp, Dianne, 'A Refutation of the Myth of the Giant Medieval Warhorse', www.florilegium.org

  'The Medieval Warhorse', www.scs.unr.edu

Karp, Dianne and Murphy, Mark, 'On the Road Medieval Style', www.florilegium.org

Keene, Dr Derek, 'Feeding Medieval European Cities, 600–1500' www.history.ac.uk

Lander, Nicholas S. 'A Memento: The Medieval Recorder', www.recorderhomepage.net

Langdale, Thomas, 'Topographical Dictionary of Yorkshire' (1822 extract), www.genuki.org.uk

Letters, Samantha, 'Online Gazetteer of Markets and Fairs in England Wales to 1516' (Yorkshire), Institute of Historical Research, www.history.ac.uk

Mackie, Peter, 'Late Medieval Taxation Records', www.history.org.uk

Mayhew, Nicholas, 'The Wealth of Medieval England', http://lamop.univ-paris1.fr

Nicholson, Professor Helen, Translations of various Templar related articles, www.deremilitari.org

Page, William, ed., 'The Victoria History of the County of York, volume 3', www.ads.ahds.ac.uk

Power, Eileen, 'The Wool Trade in English Medieval History', http://socserv.mcmaster.ca

Ryder, M.L., 'The History of Sheep Breeds in Britain', www.bahs.org.uk

Sohmer Tai, Emily, 'Marking Water: Piracy and Property in the Pre-Modern West', www.historycooperative.org

Stanford, Frank, 'The Ornithology of Anglo-Saxon England', Ða Engliscan Gesiðas Handboc, www.tha-engliscan-gesithas.org.uk

Stiles, Paula, 'Medieval Piracy and Privateering : Piracy from Pompeii to the Knights of Malta,'http://medievalhistory.suite101.com

Swicegood, John, 'The Musical Influence of Eleanor of Aquitaine', www.vanderbilt.edu

Tanner, Norman P., ed., 'Council of Vienne' from Decrees of the Ecumenical Councils, www.piar.hu

Tillotson, Dr Dianne, 'Medieval Writing', www.medievalwriting.50megs.com

Van de Noort, Robert, 'The Humber Wetland Survey: Vale of York Region', www.eng-h.gov.uk

OTHER WEBSITES

ABC National Radio ('Crusader Medicine – Interview with Dr Piers Mitchell'), www.abc.net

A Vision of Britain Through Time (North Ferriby and Wetherby), www.visionofbritain.org.uk

Access to Archives, www.a2a.org.uk

All Empires History Forum ('Crusades in the Middle East: the Impact of the Holy Land Crusades on Europe'), www.allempires.com

All Saints Church, http://swansys.co.uk/allsaints

An Open Door to the Arab World, www.al-bab.com

Archaeological Data Service, http://ads.ahds.ac.uk

Associated British Ports, Humber Estuary Services, www.humber.com

Battlefields Trust ('Battle of Northallerton'), www.battlefieldstrust.com

British Agricultural History Society, 'The Climate of Eastern England 1250–1350', www.bahs.org.uk

British History Online, www.british-history.ac.uk

British Library, www.bl.uk

Brogdale Horticultural Trust, www.brogdale.org

Catholic Encyclopedia, www.newadvent.org/cathen

Cistercians in Yorkshire, http://cistercians.shef.ac.uk

City of York Council, www.york.gov.uk/planning/localplan

Classic Encyclopedia, www.1911encyclopedia.org

Cottingley Village History Society, www.cottingleyconnect.org.uk/history

Cotton Town (Blackburn with Darwen), www.cottontown.org

Council for British Archaeology, www.britarch.ac.uk

Department for Environment Food and Rural Affairs (DEFRA), www.defra.gov.uk

East Cowton, www.eastcowton.org.uk

East Riding of Yorkshire Council, www.eastriding.gov.uk

Encyclopedia of Death and Dying www.deathreference.com

English Heritage, http://www.eng-h.gov.uk

English Heritage PastScape, http://pastscape.english-heritage.org.uk

Essential Architecture, www.essential-architecture.com

Exploratorium, the museum of science, art and human perception, www.exploratorium.edu

Fordham University, ('Medieval Sourcebook'), www.fordham.edu

Forestry Commission, www.forestry.gov.uk/dalbyforest

Geocities ('A brief history of South Cowton'), www.geocities.com

Harrogate Borough Council ('Harrogate District Landscape Character Assessment'), www.harrogate.gov.uk

Historic Hereford On Line, www.smr.herefordshire.gov.uk

History Learning Site, www.historylearningsite.co.uk

Iowa State University ('A Guide to Medieval and Renaissance Instruments'), www.music.iastate.edu

Island Net, 'The Weather Doctor', www.islandnet.com

Leeds City Council, www.leeds.gov.uk

Local Heritage Initiative, www.lhi.org.uk

Lockton and Levisham villages, www.locktonlevisham.co.uk

Medieval Cookery, www.medievalcookery.com

Medieval Life, www.medieval-life.net

Medieval World, http://medieval.etrusia.co.uk

Middle Ages ('Spices in the Middle Ages'), www.middle-ages.org.uk
Middleham, North Yorkshire, www.middlehamonline.com
Missouri State University ('Maps of Medieval Trade Routes'),
   http://history.missouristate.edu
Natural England, www.countryside.gov.uk
New Scientist Environment, http://environment.newscientist.com
North Yorkshire Moors Association, www.north-yorkshire-moors.org.uk
Out of Oblivion, www.outofoblivion.org.uk
Parish of Ebberston with Yedingham, North Yorkshire, www.ebberston.com
Portable Antiquities Scheme ('Late Medieval Mints'), www.finds.org.uk/
Prebendal Manor House, www.prebendal-manor.demon.co.uk
Real Ale ('A potted history of British ale'), www.realale.com
Romans in Britain, www.romans-in-britain.org.uk
Royal Society for the Protection of Birds, www.rspb.org.uk
Ryedale On The Net, www.ryedale.co.uk
Science Daily, www.sciencedaily.com
Snainton Parish Council, www.snaintonvillage.co.uk
South Cave Parish Council, www.southcavepc.gov.uk
South Holland Internal Drainage Board, www.south-holland-idb.gov.uk/history
Templar History Magazine, www.templarhistory.com
Temple Church London, www.templechurch.com/pages/history
Think Quest Library ('Music History'), http://library.thinkquest.org
University of Oxford ('The Fate of the Templars in Britain') http://users.ox.ac.uk
University of Texas at Austin ('Perry-Castañeda Library Map Collection Historical
   Maps of Europe'), www.lib.utexas.edu
US National Archives and Records Administration, www.archives.gov
USA Today, www.usatoday.com
Westerdale News, http://westerdale.info
Witchcraft and Wicca with Welsh Paganism, www. tylwythteg.com/templar
Women in World History www.womeninworldhistory.com
Yorkshire Archaeological Society ('A Brief Chronology of Leeds'),
   www.laplata.co.uk/thoresby/chronology
Yorkshire Dales National Park Authority, www.yorkshiredales.org.uk
Yorkshire Heritage ('Guide to Wensleydale'), www.yorkshireheritage.org.uk
Yorkshire History, www.yorkshirehistory.com
Young People's Trust for the Environment ('Britain's Disappearing Wildlife'),
   www.yptenc.org.uk